LOVE:

WITH OR WITHOUT SEX?

*The things you would want to know
about love and sex
but might not know how to ask*

CORNELIUS UCHE OKEKE

Nihil Obstat

Very Rev. Msgr. Jerome Madueke
Fides Communications, Okpuno.

Imprimatur

+ Simon A. Okafor
Bishop of Awka

First Published in Nigeria in 2005
Reprinted in 2015 by
GiPi Publications, Abuja
Plot 701 Mabushi, Cadastral Zone B6,
P.O. Box 7881 Wuse,
Abuja

ISBN-13: 978-978-53198-3-5

FOREWORD

This small book takes on a big question: should I have sex or should I wait? This question can be all-consuming, especially to young people caught in the throes of a romantic relationship. Unlike other books and materials that I have seen, this book handles the issue of chastity versus "sex" in a thoroughly intellectual, spiritual and genuine way. Rather than employing the typical "scare tactics" or "preachy" approaches, Father Okeke asks us only to be true to who we really are. As humans we are body and spirit. We are sexual creatures and we are also Divine creations. The answer to whether or not we should become sexually active in a relationship must come from a place of truth within us. How do we reconcile our heartfelt longings with the social and religious norms we have been taught?

Father Okeke's gift to us, in this small book, is to help us understand all of the pitfalls and possibilities inherent in romantic relationship. When we truly understand a choice we make, it is much easier to turn that choice into a commitment that we can keep.

Susan Chae
Attorney at Law,
Waterford, Michigan.

INTRODUCTION

Every human being yearns for relationship, because we feel that life would not have much meaning if we do not experience love from and towards our fellow human beings. Yet, relationship itself is not always an easy experience, and the love relationship between opposite sexes, which we generally call romantic love, is particularly difficult and full of conflicts and confusion. Some people are so scared of it that they are careful to the point of paralysis. Others have jumped into it and, having burned their fingers and toes, they suspect any subsequent developing relationship. There are still some others who protect themselves from romantic relationship through religious and moral laws that they very rarely reflect about. And there are others who tell the glorious tale of the joys and sorrows, challenges and painful growth experienced in love.

The story is the same all over the world because everywhere in the world people throughout the ages have engaged in love, sex, and relationships. What seems to be different from one generation to another is the understanding of and the manner in which people engage in them. For instance, the way the generations of your grandparents and your parents understand relationship, love and sex may well differ from the way your generation understands and handles them. Whatever the difference, the one thing that is common in each age is that love, sex, and relationship evoke conflicting ideas and feelings. People go through varied experiences when they enter into love relationships. They experience mystery, fear, pleasure, confusion, joy, disgust, trust, distrust, togetherness, loneliness, disappointment, fulfilment, growth, and so on. Some of these experiences are more frequent in one generation than in another, and in some relationships than in others.

A very important question that bothers every one of us, especially teenagers and younger men and women in relationship is: should the love that exists between a teenage boy and a teenage girl, a young man and a young woman, include sex or not? In other words, where do love and sex meet? Does one necessarily include or exclude the other? This problem is felt by many but expressed by only a few, and the question is more urgent when we fall in love, and we want the beloved and the lover badly. This strong drive runs in conflict with the social, moral, and religious norms that prohibit unlawful or immoral expression of sexual feelings. In that sense, this question expresses ambivalent feelings about love. Also, and more than anything, the question expresses the unease we feel in relating with the opposite sex. It captures the fears and the preoccupations that may besiege a relationship to the extent that those in it might not have time for the relationship itself. When teenagers and young people fall in love, their minds could be so preoccupied with this question that little freedom is experienced. Over and above all, this preoccupation may not allow the persons to have time to learn, study, and enjoy each other. They may remain superficial to each other for years because they are still fighting over one issue: should we have sex or not?

Some believe that sex is an integral part of a love relationship in all situations; others believe that it is not, and accept the social and religious standards that permit sexual expression only in marriage. However, not infrequently does it happen that those who readily say that sex should not be part of love except in marriage are often not fully convinced in their beliefs; they seem to repeat what their parents told them or what they learned from the catechism classes or from the Girls Guild or the Mary League Association. While their belief is good in itself, it still creates an internal conflict for them, especially when they meet fellow students in school, many of them good Christians, who say and live the opposite of the accepted social and religious norms. Then they battle over two teachings in their heads without any clear direction on how to resolve this conflict. Still, there is the third group which stands in between because it is not clear whether sex and love should go together or not.

Whichever position we take, we cannot deny the fact that this struggle is real. First, the feelings of love for the other are not disembodied feelings; they send sensations throughout the whole person, and this is felt physically in the sexual desire. The struggle is real again because the sensations felt in the body cannot be simply reduced to the effect of hormones that respond to the determination of cause and effect, tension and release. These feelings, though embodied, are the feelings of a human subject who has a self that is not explained totally by hormones, nerves, and arteries. This is why love, sex, and relationships are not as simple as they may sometimes suggest. We experience the complexity in our own personal lives especially when we fall in love.

I have had the opportunity to speak to young people on some occasions about love and sex. Many of their questions revolve around the place of sex in a love relationship. At some point, one could get the impression that these young people are asking for permission to do what they feel in their hearts or what they think "feels right". It can be a frustrating experience that feels like a dilemma.

My intention in writing this book is to explore this question in a way that will engage you the reader. In these pages I try to speak directly to you, to your feelings, personal experiences in your relationships, and the experiences of others who may or may not be close to you. These feelings and experiences are the first data we have before us. I shall take you a step further in understanding them; that is, trying to sift out what these experiences and feelings are saying. Then it is hoped you will be able to give a personal response to the question: how do sex and love relate. You will notice in these pages that all the difficulties we experience in a love relationship stem from ourselves. They derive from the levels of our psychosocial immaturity and ignorance. There is, therefore, the need to grow in maturity and self-knowledge to be able to have an enriching love relationship.

This work is divided into two parts. In the first part, I shall address the relationship between sex and erotic or romantic love. This part shall examine the meaning of sex, sexuality, relationship, and the experience of erotic love. The second part takes the desires of Eros beyond itself to the deepest desire of the human heart where we all yearn for a love that endures forever. This part shall explore the relationship between our yearnings for love and yearnings for God; the lights and shadows of love, the influence of human weakness in loving, and how the power of love serves our growth, especially if we respond to the deepest desire of the human spirit.

The desire to write this book came from two sources. First, it came from the talks I gave to the Catholic students of Nnamdi Azikiwe University, Nigeria, in 2004, and the questions they raised.

Secondly, it came from the questions the students of John Paul II Major Seminary, Awka, Nigeria, raised during my lectures on the Psychology of Human Development. This book is an effort to clarify these questions in a more systematic manner. I thank them for their questions, and I hope the contents of this book will address at least some of them.

In February 2005, I became very sick and went to the United States for medical treatment. During that period, I was hosted by my dear friend, Fr. Douglas Bignall, in the rectory of St. Angela Parish, Roseville, Michigan. It was during this period that I started putting these ideas down. I thank him for his hospitality and generosity. I thank his parishioners for their kindness towards me. I remain grateful to the staff and students of Pope John Paul II Major Seminary for their prayers and support especially during this time of my sickness.

When I needed to read some books on the topic while I shuttled from one doctor to another, it was Wanda Edie, a friend and a mother, who provided me with some of the books. She also read the manuscript and offered her invaluable remarks. I am grateful to her for this and for her undiminished support. My friends, Matt and Carol Fett, also provided me with some books and read the manuscript. I thank them a lot for their love and for supporting me in the publication of this work. I also thank Bill Terrien for his insights after reading the manuscript. Your corrections and comments were very helpful. In a very special way I am grateful to Susan Chae who read the manuscript very critically, edited it, and accepted to write the foreword. I appreciate it a lot.

I am grateful to Very Rev. Msgr. Jerome Madueke for going through the manuscript and making important remarks about it. Fr. Lawrence Nwankwo has been a very supportive friend. He read the manuscript critically and offered invaluable comments that improved the quality of the argument and the presentation. I really thank him. And to my bishop, Most Rev. Simon Okafor, I remain grateful for his paternal support.

In a special way I thank Sr. Ifeoma who called me many times during this period of my sickness to ask how I was doing. Your jokes and stories lifted my spirit. In the same way I thank Uzoma, a great friend, who, though far away back in Nigeria, checked on me with love. I thank all my friends, men and women, for your love and the lessons of our friendship. I dedicate this book to the teenagers, men and women, young and old, who struggle to make sense of their experiences of love. If this book helps you in anyway, then my joy in writing it is complete.

Cornelius Uche Okeke
August 25, 2005.

TABLE OF CONTENT

Part II: The transformation of romantic lovers and their love

Chapter Five:
Love struggles with the weakness of human nature

Chapter Six:
From romance to committed love

Conclusion

Part I

Love and Sex: the Height and the Depth

Chapter One

Relationship, Love and Sex: Essential Facts

Relationship: Primary and Secondary

We need to start with examining the meaning of relationship because love and sex take place in the context of a relationship.

Relationship is the state of being connected or related. In general it describes what is happening between two or more events, objects or persons, how they are related. For instance, there is a relationship between oxygen and hydrogen in that both are connected in the formation of water. In the same way we can say there is a relationship between mosquito and malaria, because the parasites carried by mosquitoes lead to malaria. We can also assume there is a relationship, for example, between cheating on exams and irresponsibility, because a large number of people who tend to cheat in exams tend to be irresponsible in some other areas of their lives.

These examples illustrate a general sense in which relationships can be understood.

When a relationship exists between persons it is called an *interpersonal* relationship. It means that the persons, two or more, are connected to each other in a certain way. Relationships among human beings may be divided into *primary* and *secondary* interpersonal relationships. Primary interpersonal relationship means "a basic, long-lasting relationship founded upon strong emotional ties and a sense of commitment to the other person"[1]. Notice the emphasis on *emotion* and *commitment*. The reason is because people in such relationships tend to know each other very well because they have shared their stories many times and revealed themselves in many ways. The people in a primary relationship have become bonded to each other to such an extent that the manner of relating is informal, diffuse and less boundary-conscious.

In primary relationships, one member cannot replace the other essentially because of the emotional tie and commitment. A typical example is a woman whose husband died when she was 35. She refused to marry again because she felt she could not love another man as she loved her late husband. People kept telling her to forget about her husband and make a choice among the many men who were asking her to marry them. Such statements betray our ignorance of the structure and dynamics of a primary relationship. For this woman, there are many men but her husband was not just any man; he was *the* man, the love of her life. Again, we often hear it said that there are many women out there for one to choose from. This is simply untrue if one is looking for a woman to love and live with forever as a wife, which would involve some deep emotional bonding. People in primary relationship cannot easily replace each other without some kind of emotional strain.

Secondary relationship between persons is relatively short-lived and is generally characterized by formal and limited interaction. Moreover, the persons in it are generally very conscious of the boundary that exists between them. Emotional involvement is often lacking or is at least limited, and the participants in such a relationship can be replaced by another. This is the way we generally relate to most classmates, colleagues at work, or the many acquaintances we have. In such a relationship, little of our personal story is revealed. When persons in a secondary relationship miss each other in the case of separation, it is usually for the services or help they might have rendered mutually to each other. This is what happens when the director of a company misses his sales manager who died, because he is competent at his job; or a student misses a fellow student who helps him or her in studies. When persons in a secondary relationship move on to another place or take on a new assignment or job, they form new relationships with the new colleagues. They can be forgotten by previous colleagues or remembered for their goodness or competence at work or school.

You will have noticed that problems will ensue when people are unable to know which kind of relationship exists between them and others. It is a problem that young and old people experience in various forms. It is present in relationships among boys or girls, and between boys and girls, men and women. People do not tell us whether they are in primary or secondary relationship with us; they simply show it in their behaviour.

Take the example of Agatha who is relating with Rose, a fellow student. Rose tells Agatha everything about herself, her family, the most significant experiences she has had, the hurts in her life. Agatha simply listens and consoles Rose, but is unwilling to reveal herself. Rose likes Agatha a lot and wants to have more time with her, but Agatha hardly visits Rose, even though they are in the same school. One day, Rose is angry and feels that Agatha is mean and without feeling. She goes and tells Njide who is from her town. The only thing that connects her with Njide is that they come from the same town. Njide tells Rose that her accusation of Agatha may not really be true; it could be that Agatha does not want any emotional bonding with Rose. But Rose wants Agatha. One day she comes up with a wise idea to ask Agatha about their relationship. She goes to Agatha and says to her: "It seems I'm bothering you in this relationship!" Agatha politely replied: "Not really".

She may not have the courage to say clearly what their relationship means to her, but Rose is wise enough to get the message: "she does not want to get deep in this relationship with me". How does she know this? Because "not really" is a polite and cold response; it does not express anything concrete. It is now up to Rose to decide whether she accepts to relate with Agatha at a less intimate level. Suppose Rose does not get the message, as most of us hardly do. What will happen to her? Two alternatives: first, she will be on Agatha's back, calling her names. She loses her peace because she is frustrated. In the meantime Agatha goes on with her life. Or, Rose might decide to coerce Agatha to relate with her at the level she wants by being nice to Agatha, buying her things and rendering certain services to her. Agatha might be nice to her as well, but without serious emotional ties. After a long period of no success, Rose might start to gossip about Agatha, so that there might be some minor or major conflicts between them. These are ways Rose tries desperately to express her frustration. The method she adopts to handle the problem depends on her personality and temperament.

This structure of a relationship I have described between Rose and Agatha is experienced within and across sexes. Most of us in one way or another have fallen into that blind alley where we think a primary relationship exists when all that is there is a secondary relationship, and it is always frustrating.

You see why it is important to know the nature of the relationship between you and others. This will help you understand your feelings. There are persons you may want to have a relationship with at the primary level, but they want to relate with you at a secondary level. Sometimes it is difficult to understand this, and at other times, it is hard to accept it because of the hope you entertain that such a person in your life will make your life more meaningful: he or she will make you feel good about yourself; relationship with that person will increase your self-esteem; and so on. We are not usually aware of these expectations, but they cause us a lot of trouble in our relationships because they are the very forces which drive us to frustration when we do not get what we expect in a relationship. Secondly, these expectations are the source of disappointments and deep hurts. If you realize that a person relates with you at the secondary level, and you insist he or she relates at the primary level, and it does not happen, you need to make a decision: either to keep it at the level the other feels comfortable, or if you cannot bear it, you can quit the relationship in a gentle way. It is impossible to relate with everyone at the primary level. That is simply the way it is with all of us. Be aware of this distinction for you will see a lot of implications it has in our experience of love.

Love

Everyone has his or her own understanding of love, and we try to bring this understanding into our relationships. For some people love is simply feeling good about oneself before another; it is to experience that the other person cares for *me*. For others, it is just "being adored" by another. Yet, to some others, it is sharing everything with the beloved. Whatever the differences in understanding, love is understood generally as an "intense feeling of deep affection or fondness for a person or a thing"[2]; "a great attachment to and affection for something or person"[3]; "an intense feeling of strong liking or affection for some specific thing or person; an enduring sentiment toward a person producing a desire to be with that person and a concern for the happiness and satisfactions of that person"[4]. Note that the recurring term in these descriptions is *affection*. It is what the heart feels towards a person; it is an *affective state* that influences all interactions with, and perceptions of, the person loved. This shows that love is known better when it is experienced.

Human experience has shown that there are different kinds of love because different persons and the relationships we have with them evoke different kinds of *affective states* in us. That is, we feel differently towards certain persons. Everyone knows this, but it was the Greeks who were the first to give names to these affective states or loves.

Storgē or Domestic Love

There is the love among members of a family in which each one is bound to another by birth, mutual care and attention. This is called domestic love and it is understood in all families of the world. We have affection for the members of our family and this usually includes our extended family in our African culture. Parents take care of their children and their children take care of them. Because of this emotional bond, an Igbo proverb holds that the anger of a brother or sister does not reach the bone (*Iwe nwanne anaghị eru n'ọkpụkpụ*). On certain occasions, however, precisely because the hurt comes from a brother or sister, it easily touches the bone. The love of our family members is the first experience of our safety and security in the world, and from them we have our first awareness of our loveliness which is the foundation of our self-esteem. We all need that safe home or family in order to start the long and arduous journey of life. When life proves too tough and unbearable, we usually bounce back to it in order to set off again on the journey. When love is lacking in our development, life itself can constitute an unusual problem: those who feel they have not been loved enough can be terribly wounded in their lives; they easily feel rejected and unloved so deeply that they may spend most of their lives looking for this love.

Eros or Romantic Love

We also recognize that we have a different feeling toward a man or a woman we care for or feel attracted to. Sometimes we try to make that person notice us and admire us with the hope that one day, providence will bring us together to interact, and verbalize our feelings. A young woman usually prays that God touches the young man she cares for so that, at least, he can ask her even for a pencil to write with in school. That will give her the opportunity to put up certain attitudes that will set the man thinking about her. From then on, she will be on the look out for any indication that he is interested. When she is convinced that her bait has him, she will draw from her God-given talents to make sure that his interest increases every day. A man, on the other hand, usually is not patient to pray for providence when he notices a woman he likes. He goes out to meet her and asks providence to confirm his effort. Having 'conquered' the woman, he does everything within his power to keep her to himself. In the meantime, a whole set of new feelings toward themselves has emerged: they have fallen in love, and life has changed. Their feeling for each other is so strong that it can disrupt their normal day to day lives. But the lovers do not care; nothing is more important than the feelings they are experiencing for each other. For these two lovers, the sun shines in a new way and the darkness of the night has lost its scare; life takes on a new significance. It is like their whole world revolves around this experience: they dream dreams about each other, talk often about their new experience, and desire to see each other constantly. They experience joy and peace for having found the love of their lives, and they want to hold themselves closely and permanently.

When these things are going on between man and woman, it is the force of *eros* that is at work. It is that love that pulls a man and a woman together, expressing the deep yearning for union, completion and procreation. This desire for union tends to seek expression in sexual intercourse; hence the predominant identification of Eros with sexual love[5]. Whenever we talk of love, this is what most of us know, and most of the books on love deal with this love. It is the prototype of human experience of love, and it is this that brings so much joy and so much pain, delight and anguish. And when it is allied with sex, it can lead both to rapture and anxiety.

This love is called romantic or erotic love. Though the word *erotic* derives from this love, its identification with sex is not totally correct. As we shall see in this study, the love that is experienced in *eros* is characterized principally by a heightened preoccupation with the beloved. Sex is usually secondary in *eros*, and when it does take place, it is often unintended, and does not carry the weight of that concupiscence that permeates the thinking and actions of the man or woman driven by sexual desire. When sex is the preoccupation in a relationship, it is certainly not *eros* that is at work.

Philia or Friendship

There is also the love that exists among members of the same sex, and also between the sexes. It is a love characterized by affection and concern. We usually describe this love as brotherly or sisterly love. This kind of relationship evokes feelings that are certainly different from the ones we have toward family members or toward the beloved in a romantic love. This is the relationship the Greeks specifically call friendship and its name is *Philia*. It expresses the love between friends or even "the love of husband and of wife"[6]. Friends share common ideals, convictions and values, and help each other in pursuing life goals. They share each other's painful and joyful moments. Friends know each other deeply. Philia is a lovely word that expresses "warmth and closeness and affection"[7], and it is usually not besieged by the kind of intense and disrupting feelings of Eros.

Philia or friendship among members of the same sex is not the same thing as homosexuality or lesbianism. In homosexual and lesbian relationships the central factor is the sexual orientation of those involved. That is why homosexuality is distinguished from heterosexuality in terms of sexual inclinations. Philia is concerned with shared vision and mutual readiness to accompany each other through life's struggles and challenges.

Agape or Charity

There are times in which we are so touched with the condition of another that we are moved to show love even when ordinarily we would not do that. For instance, imagine the situation in which a man from your village plans with some others and takes some portion of your land just because your Dad is no longer alive. You feel helpless and you wait for the day to come when you will avenge for this aggression against your family. As time passes, you find yourself in the same university with a son of this man, and he is in a difficult academic situation, and you can help him. Though you feel the rage against his family and think about revenge, you do not act on the feeling of vengeance but you go out of your way to assist this young man. When you get back to your room you ask yourself: "How was I able to do that? How could I do this with all the anger in me?" This love you showed to the young man despite the resistance you felt inside is what the Greeks call *agape*. It is called *caritas* in Latin or charity in English. It is the love which is devoted to the welfare of the other; it is that disposition to love the other for his or her sake without any gain or ulterior motive. The prototype of this love is seen in God's love for us human beings when He sent his son, Jesus Christ, to die for us, even when we don't appreciate it. This is the kind of love that inspires us when we forgive and perform deeds of love towards persons who commit atrocities against us. It is that love by which we love and care for those who do not love us, those who may even be our enemies. This is why *agape* is not simply emotion; it is more of a principle we live by; it is "a deliberate principle of the mind, and a deliberate conquest and achievement of the will. It is in fact the power to love the unlovable, to love people whom we do not like"[8].

C.S. Lewis, the famous English writer, pointed out that the one thing the first three loves – *storgē*, *eros* and *philia* – have in common is that they are meant to satisfy the needs of the persons involved in them: members of family love each other and take care of themselves; the man and woman involved in romantic love are concerned with loving themselves and being loved; friends help each other. For this reason, he calls these three loves Need-Love. This implies that it is hard for human beings to love in a totally unselfish way. He describes *agape* as Gift-Love because what motivates the lover in agape is the giving of him or herself completely to a person without any gain, as in the example given in the last paragraph. That is why it is more an act of the will than of emotion.

Agape is the finest love and a great human experience because people grow to the fullness of themselves the more they can forget themselves and seek the good of others. All of us usually start life with being concerned with our needs, our safety, our comfort, our pleasures, as little children and as teenagers. But we grow in life and through life weaning ourselves of too much self-preoccupation in order to serve others. Psychologists agree that people are more mature the more they have learned to consider the needs of others as being very important rather than focusing solely on their own needs. People who are too preoccupied with themselves, the way they look, their popularity, how many people love them, are often called narcissists.

Narcissism came from the story of Narcissus who was the son of a river god, Cephissus. He was a young man of incredible beauty and elegance. But he was also vain, so vain that Echo, a female mountain nymph fell in love with him. But he was cold to her; he disregarded her love. Echo suffered so much from this cold response of Narcissus that the god Nemesis decided to punish Narcissus for his vanity. What was the punishment? He made Narcissus drink at a pool of water. When he bent down to drink from that pool, Narcissus saw a reflection of his beauty and fell in love with it; that is, he fell in love with himself. From then onwards, he became so obsessed with himself that he eventually wasted away. Get the message:

Narcissus became so preoccupied with himself that no other person mattered. Narcissists are people who are so worried about their needs and desires that they use other persons to satisfy themselves. We all behave like that in many ways especially in our love relationships. But the more we grow and mature, the more we learn to do things for others and to love people for their sake rather than for our own good, comfort or any other ulterior motive. This is what C.S. Lewis means when he observed that all Need-Love grows and weeds itself of the compulsive neediness and matures into Gift-Love. We have to remember, however, that in every love there is always a give and take. But it depends on which one predominates: whether it is the giving or the taking. The basic challenge is to grow in giving of ourselves. 'Giving' not simply of what we have but of ourselves. This implies that we are engaged in the project of building up ourselves psychologically, morally, spiritually, in order to be able to give ourselves as gifts to others.

You must have noticed that whenever we are talking of love, we are talking of the primary relationship in the strict sense of it. In every form of love, there is an affective state, an emotional bonding and commitment, which are the characteristics of a primary relationship. Though agape does not portray strong emotions as in *storge*, *eros* and *philia*, the person who lives it believes in the principle, which is why his will responds to it. Our convictions and principles are our values and whenever they become important to us, they carry emotions. Mother Theresa's love for the poor and abandoned children of Calcutta was an act of the will, a decision, but also a principle she lived by, a value that was so important to her because it is personified in Jesus Christ, whom she loved tremendously.

I have examined the four kinds of love and their meanings. Each of them has a different object and a specific form of affective state that distinguishes it from the others. As you may have noticed, the question of the relationship between love and sex is posed usually in Eros more than in any other kind of love. Before I get into the detailed discussion of it in the later chapters, I need to clarify your ideas about sex and sexuality.

Sexuality and Sex

In a general sense, sexuality expresses that power we have to relate with fellow human beings, God, and the universe. It is the passion which enables us to establish and sustain relationships. It is that fire that burns constantly within us and compels us "to turn toward one another"[9], and to God. That is why some persons can devote their lives in the service of other human beings solely for their love for God and for others. Anyone who loves God and lives an intense spiritual life knows that he or she experiences stirrings of love in their heart that can be expressed almost in the same manner that couples in love express themselves. It is for this reason that mystics employ the language of sexual union to express their relationship with God, as in the Song of Songs. In this sense, sexuality is truly our love energy[10].

More specifically, sexuality is an umbrella word which encompasses first, our sexual anatomy, whether we are male or female which is determined by our sexual organs and body structure. These determine our sexual identity. Secondly, the word also expresses our psychology, that is, the way we perceive and think about being male or female. This is expressed in our gender behaviours and attitudes, whether we behave as men or as women. All this put together constitutes what is referred to as gender identity[11]. A person may be a man from the appearance of his sexual organ but feels and behaves like a woman. There are also some women whose physical structures and sexual organs indicate that they are women, but who feel and behave like men. Such people suffer what we call gender identity disorder. This means that their feelings about themselves do not match with their sexual identities.

In determining gender identity, socio-cultural elements come into play because different cultures have different ways of raising boys and girls. This means that cultures prescribe acceptable sexual and gender behaviours for both sexes. For instance, in Igbo culture, people frown at a woman who sits with her legs apart "like a man", they will say, even if she is wearing a pair of trousers; this is usually not seen in Western Europe or North America where women can wear a dress or trousers freely and sit any way they want. Secondly, it is generally assumed in most cultures that it is males who have to seek and conquer females so that sexual activities have to be initiated by the males. At the same time, seductiveness is associated with being female, so that women seek to dress in such a way as to attract attention.

Whatever the differences in raising males and females in various cultures are, it is not contestable that the anatomical differences between men and women express an ontological difference between them; a difference not of opposition but of complimentarity and relationship[12]. It is a misdirected opinion to think, as some authors do[13], that gender difference is largely a cultural or social construct and, therefore, people should free themselves from it. This kind of thinking has ruined many a man and many a woman and destabilized the ontological basis of a healthy relationship between the sexes which is visibly expressed in their different anatomies. Though some gender roles could be culture-specific, and sometimes even oppressive, this does not annul or render baseless the biologically determined structures and their psychological implications for men and women.

In recent times, sexual orientation is also included in the concept of sexuality[14]. It refers to "a person's erotic response tendency – homosexual, bisexual, or heterosexual – toward other persons of the same or other sex as reflected in such indicators as the proportion of dreams and fantasies directed to one or the other sex, the sex of one's sexual partners, and the extent of physiological response to erotic stimuli associated with one or both genders"[15]. These aspects of sexuality are summarized in Reber's definition of sexuality as "all those aspects of one's constitution and one's behaviour that are related to sex"[16]. In this more specific sense, sexuality therefore connotes all those things that make us sexual beings, male and female, and the sexual activities through which we express them.

Sex on the other hand can mean two things. First, it means our biological make up definable by the appearance of the genital organs. In this sense we talk of male sex or female sex. When a woman gives birth to a child, we usually ask "male or female?" and the answer comes from the genitals. Secondly, Sex is used as a short term for sexual intercourse, as when one is said to have sex. This second meaning includes the feelings or behaviors resulting from the urge to gratify the sexual desire. It embraces "arousal and activities associated with sexual feelings, fantasies, masturbation, foreplay or intercourse for the purpose of pleasure and/or reproduction"[17].

Some people can engage in sex solely to gratify their sexual need or to have children or both. This means that sex does not necessarily imply an emotional tie or bond between the two persons; it can take place without any deep emotional tie or relationship. Human experience testifies to this. People do engage in sex whether they are in love or not, hence, the existence of such expression as *loveless sex*. Examples of loveless sex include rape, incest, solitary sex as in masturbation, and prostitution in its obvious form such as in professional prostitution, and the less obvious form such as the sexual alliance with sugar daddies and sugar mommies. There is also the example of powerful people who take advantage of persons in vulnerable situations to gratify their sexual desires. Take the example of the teachers or lecturers who have the habit of passing female or male students in the exams on the condition that the students go to bed with them. Some students accept this deal, and it has become the easiest way for them to get a degree they did not study for. Another example: a rich man in the village pays the school fees of a widow's children as long as she sleeps with him. At some point, her eldest daughter joins in paying sexual tribute to the rich man.

In these examples the main focus is the satisfaction of the sexual desire. These things happen all over the world though the form it takes varies from place to place.

There is also the engagement in sex for the sake of having children. In different parts of Africa, to have children is a primary reason to get married.

Despite the influence of European culture, this reason for marriage is still very strong in many African countries and ethnic groups. Moreover, in many ethnic groups, such as the Igbo, to be a married man or woman forms an integral part of a person's self-esteem. This situation leads to people getting married just because they think they should get married. And often, they may not marry the man or the woman they can say they really love. Some marry out of desperation and are content to have children. Sometimes such married people engage in sex because it is legally allowed for the sake of children, and not because they deeply care for one another, so that when they have their last baby, they may tend to lose interest in each other. Or, it can happen that they meet sexually in order to have children, and when they want to enjoy the pleasure of sex itself, they meet the person they feel some affection for, depending on the level of moral sensitivity. Some lose interest in sex completely and are simply happy they are mothers and fathers. There are some men and women who are so driven with sexual desire that it does not matter to them who is available to fulfil it. This can happen within and outside marriage.

All we have been discussing so far should be able to show you that relationships, love and sex are complex. There are many issues that are involved of which a lot of people are unaware. In the next chapter I shall draw your attention further to the conscious and unconscious reasons why people have sex, and the confusion this could create in relationship and love.

.

Chapter Two

Attraction and Ambiguity in Sex

The Mystery of Sexual Desire

There is something mysterious about sexual desire which makes it an important theme of songwriters, poets, musicians and even academics, philosophers, and theologians. Every generation and every culture experiences fascination about the pleasures of sex. The experience tends to reduce everything and every other desire almost irrelevant in that single moment in which it would seem the heavens touch the earth. But above all, it is that intense pleasure by means of which each of us came into the world, and through which future generations of the human race shall be born. Yet, it is "the source at once of the human being's most intense pleasure and his most pervasive anxiety. It can, in its daimonic form, hurl the individual into sloughs of despond, and, when allied with eros, it can lift him out of despondency into orbits of ecstasy"[1].

An important indication of this mystery in sexual desire is that there is something in it that radiates into man's psychological life "that is shared neither by the desire to eat nor by the pleasure that the satisfaction of this desire procures. Above all, sexual ecstasy goes to the very depth of bodily existence; it has in its overwhelming power something extraordinary, to which terrible bodily pains are alone a counterpart"[2]. This is to say that sexual desire is not like any desire: it is not like the desire to eat or drink. Though it is mostly a bodily experience, it goes beyond that into the depth of our whole being because it includes intentionality, a response to another who is a person with body, soul and spirit[3]. These constitute the "very depth of our embodied existence". The sexual instinct is present in all animals, but in the human being, it is more than an instinct: it cuts through a person's body and penetrates every dimension of his or her life: the psychic and the spiritual. In the words of Julius Evola, sex in human beings is free from the "bonds and seasonal periods of sexual excitement that are maintained in animal sexuality"[4] because sexual desire in human beings is substantially psychic in nature; that is, it expresses the whole person and not just his or her biology.

This is the basic reason why sex is both a source of pleasure and anxiety, and indeed a problem that philosophers and theologians, starting from Plato through Avicenna to Thomas Aquinas, down to the contemporary world, have grappled with. And the problem is how to enable sexual desire and sexual act which we share in common with animals to express and facilitate our humanity and not fracture it. The problem is real because whenever sexual desire is lived wholly as a mere bodily activity, as a plaything or a sport, it can be a source of pleasure and relaxation for the moment, but retains the power to alienate the individual from within the depth of his or her being. It can express union with the other but, at the same time, it can bring persons to the experience of utter loneliness.

Thus sex in the human being expresses both attraction and ambiguity. In its attraction, sex is pleasurable, and tends to raise our hopes and expectations for a better life, for love, and for delight. But sex is also ambiguous because people can use it to express known and unknown desires that have little or no relationship to love or affection.

The Ambiguity in Sex

Human beings are mysteries themselves so that sometimes, if not most of the time, what they present as their question and their desire may mask the true question and the true desire. Take the example of Johnson and Linda who come together for the sole purpose of praying and studying in school. This is what they tell themselves, for it is what they are aware of. They are members of the Charismatic Movement, and so are brother and sister! It does not take much time and they begin to experience excitement for each other. One day, they pray together, study together, and conclude the session with hugs, kisses, and sex. Then they exclaim that it is not their plan; that the devil is the cause. Indeed, they did not plan it, but there was no devil. Could it be that they were already attracted to each other, and the normal and unembarrassing way of getting to each other would be through praying and studying together? If they told themselves what they were feeling they might not believe they still were brother and sister. Then they left it to the unconscious to play the trick. How? Let us look at what happened.

If Linda is honest with herself she will admit that even though she prepares to go and pray with Johnson, she is also worried about how he looks at her: whether he admires her enough; whether he makes any comment that suggests she is not attractive enough. And if she gets the impression that he notices her, she dresses up to be able to stimulate and keep up the admiration. Johnson on his own part makes overtures to her but convinces himself that he is being a supporting brother. After their prayers and studies, he says to Linda: "Your prayer is as beautiful as you are!" He believes he gives her a spiritual compliment, but Linda goes home with that lavish "spiritual" compliment and turns it over in her mind. Though the compliment could appear to be spiritual, it penetrates every aspect of her being. What happens? The next time, she dresses even better and better and receives more compliments and admirations until the day they express their mutual attraction in sexual form. Only then they wake up, but not fully awake because they see the devil as the cause. They kneel down and cast out the devil together for more effectiveness. But they are still asleep. They will wake up from their sleep when they realize how their desire for one another developed and simmered but was covered with many prayers and studies. Their distractions were called temptations and therefore avoided instead of looked at, and these unknown or unconscious events eventually led to that fateful day that was blamed on the devil. Isn't this a mystery we live every day in different forms?

This example shows that our motivations are often mixed, and express our unconscious desires and unresolved conflicts. Sexual intercourse is often used to express these unconscious desires. It can be used "to express all sorts of individual conflicts, needs and concerns, rather than an affectionate, pleasurable relationship between two individuals"[5]. In other words, sex does not always express love and affection. The fundamental reason for this ambiguity is because all of us are always in search of our individual uniqueness. This uniqueness means that each of us is loveable in a very unique way. But because we do not always believe this, we are always in need of affirmation from others, so that sex can easily become an avenue to seek or express that. Secondly, the pains of growing up, the troubles of self-esteem, the tensions of living, and the agonies of rejection, are instances that question whether we are indeed loveable! Some people tend to seek an outlet to these painful experiences in the pleasures of sex. Mary Anna Friederich has identified such reasons why people have sex other than love and affection. For the sake of this reflection I have chosen to present some of them and add a few others.

Sex as a Drug

People can use sex just in the same way that drugs such as cocaine, marijuana or alcohol are used. This is what happens when people have sex in order to release anxiety and tension. In moments of great tension or anxiety some persons 'act out' the tension in sexual intercourse or in a compulsive masturbation. In either case, the sexual pleasure "is similar to 'drowning one's sorrows in alcohol,' 'taking a trip' on drugs or treating a fever with aspirin. The individual has little if any capacity to be concerned with anyone except himself or herself"[6]. In the same vein, some people engage in sexual intercourse or masturbation just to free themselves from the frustrations of life[7]. In all these instances, sex serves as a drug and not an expression of affection. A man's financial condition gets worse every day, and he feels frustrated about it. He finds himself masturbating more in this condition than before even though he is married. A student is experiencing a lot of difficulty in preparing for her exams. She vents her anger and frustration in masturbation or sexual intercourse with her boyfriend. In these instances, sexual pleasure serves as a drug, and helps them 'forget' their problems at the moment.

Sex used to get Pregnant and to prove One's Fertility

Some people engage in sexual intercourse primarily for getting pregnant and/or having a child. This is understandable in African culture, where a woman must prove that she is fertile and a man proves that he is potent. To be a mother and a father enters into the psychological identity of the African woman and man, as we said earlier in the first chapter. A couple could not have a child. Both husband and wife suspected and blamed each other. In order to prove his manhood, the man went in to another woman and made her pregnant. Now, he is happy that he is a man. Afterwards, the child was aborted. The man did not care so much about the morality of abortion because he had regained his self-esteem. In the meantime, his wife had tried her former boyfriend in secret and became pregnant and aborted it also for fear of troubles at home. She is sure now that she can conceive; she is a woman. You see that this couple is driven into these sexual acts less by sexual pleasure or affection but in order to prove their fertility. When such a need is strong, moral sensitivity can be dulled.

Sex as a Proof of One's Identity

Some people have sex in order to prove their gender identity. There are certain young men who feel they are men if they can have sex with a woman. Otherwise, they keep feeling something is wrong with them. This can be found among those young men taunted by peers for having had no sexual experience. Some of them are unable to deal with such caricatures; others are strong enough to keep to their convictions. Jonathan is an example of a young man who finds it difficult to contain the criticisms of his peers in the university. Because his peers make fun of him, he feels something is wrong with him; he begins to notice that he has become afraid of women. So, in order to prove that he is like others, first, he visits the prostitutes. He comes back feeling good. He tells his closest friend. His friend makes fun of him and tells him that it is not the same thing as conquering a girl and having sex with her. He feels bad again, and looks out for a young woman he can talk to. He succeeds and takes her to bed. And it is over. He goes to his friend and tells him of his success. He is praised for it. Now, he can feel he is a man.

In the same way, there are middle-aged men and older ones who use sexual intercourse with younger women to prove that they are still alive and have not lost their vitality as men. Some young and middle-aged women also think and behave like Jonathan. Their degree of attractiveness is proved by the extent they can seduce men who take them to bed. For such women, engaging in sexual intercourse means they are attractive to men. And this is meant to prove their feminine identity.

Sex used to prove that One is Important

Sexual intercourse, especially among women, could be used to prove that one has self-worth and value. Such women tend to be promiscuous, not because they want it, but because they are easily seduced by sweet words, which mean a lot to them. They yearn to prove their worth and value, and in this desire, they can submit themselves sexually to several men. The promiscuity is merely a symptom of the deep feelings of not-good-enough and the loneliness that goes with it. Unfortunately, the more they are promiscuous, the more lonely and insecure they feel. A woman who falls for any man does not really value herself. This is the situation of Adaobi who feels she is not good enough even though she is beautiful, intelligent, and social. But she always feels every other woman in the university is more beautiful than she is; that she has no value. Sometimes she gets in a bad mood, and a man arrives and tells her she is very important. She follows him. After a while, the man dumps her, and she is back to her problem. Just then another man surfaces, and the cycle is repeated. Adaobi becomes wayward, driven by the search for her worth.

Sex used to get Attention and Love

There are also those for whom sex is a means to get attention and love in order to escape from loneliness. Friederich believes this happens mostly among women. For instance, "in searching for affection and attention, a woman may end up having intercourse without having so planned. She may yearn for the fondling and caresses a man can give without realizing that this may sexually excite him more than herself"[8]. It happens frequently that after the event, the woman gets angry towards the man for "exploiting" her, and does not remember that she desires the touches and the fondling. Some women will tell men that the only thing they want is just touches and nothing more. And they become surprised that it leads further into sexual intercourse. On the other hand, there are men who can easily spot these young women who yearn for that attention, and they can give it abundantly. Oftentimes, these women feel like 'pleasing' the men by granting them the request for intercourse. This situation is not uncommon in the university setting where people come from their homes to a new environment, and can feel lost and unnoticed. Women especially can feel fearful and unsafe. A guy comes up with promises of protection and attention, and she gives in. Many a time, a man knows that his intention for relating to this woman is to get a sexual fix, but the woman hardly is aware of it; all she knows is that with this man, she feels protected and loved. This can lead to many unfortunate surprises.

Sex used to boost Self-Esteem

Many of us do not have very high self-esteem. But we can be aware of it, work on it, and use different healthy ways to increase it. For some people, however, sex is the available means of "feeling" they have high self-esteem, which makes it even worse. Take the example of men who boast of having conquered and slept with many women. What are they trying to express? They are trying to convince us that they are strong and able. But why do they have to convince us of it? Because they feel insecure and inadequate. People who are sure of themselves go about their business with less talk about it; they have no need to boast before others. Most of the time, the more people boast of an apparent achievement, the more they reveal the emptiness within themselves that the so-called achievement was expected to fill. This fulfilment rarely happens because the person is living a defensive life. Such people spend their lives trying to prove something to the world because they feel insecure. It is this drive to prove something that takes away the peace that they should be experiencing. And in the case of demonstrated sexual prowess, the situation is even more frustrating and emptying.

Some women also do the same when they try "to prove themselves attractive by seducing as many men as possible. Here sexuality is a way of manoeuvring another to serve one's needs"[9]. When some married women in their middle life dress seductively, they often send out the unconscious message that "'sex appeal' is a powerful force they can muster to defend against the distressing reality that they are growing older"[10]. Growing old is not easy for anyone, men and women, but in some people, it is particularly a terrible and frustrating experience that wears off layers of self-esteem. Some women then make intense efforts to prove themselves young, and their ability to appeal sexually to men becomes the easiest indication that they are succeeding. But this is a lost game for nature's clock cannot be unwound. What sadness this has left in many lives!

Sex used to express Anger

Anger and destruction could also be expressed through sexual intercourse. This can take place among married couples or among unmarried men and women. For instance, there are some women who refuse intercourse with their husbands as a kind of punishment for their bad attitudes. For many months, Felicia has been asking her husband, Sampson, to give her some money to add to the sum she has already put in her business but he is reluctant to give her any amount. Yet, he does not give her any convincing reason. She feels frustrated and angry. From the third month of this plea, she refuses intercourse with him. She simply tells him that she has a headache, and is not in the mood. After some weeks, Sampson gets very angry, and goes after another woman. To make the situation worse, he brings the woman to Felicia to "shame you to death", he says. In revenge, Felicia closes up to Sampson and goes out with a more wealthy man who provides both sex and the needed financial help. As you can see, a cycle of aggression and destruction has been put in motion, and the weapon used is sexual intercourse.

There is also the case of Bernard and Prisca who have been friends since they came into the university. They are course mates. Bernard feels Prisca does not love him enough because she is free with other men within and outside the department. She is very social, but not careless. He gets angry at the freedom of Prisca. He feels that the powerful way to express his anger toward Prisca and bend her to him is to get close to her girlfriend Janet and take her to bed. He succeeds and tells Prisca about it. Meanwhile, Janet, though a long time girlfriend of Prisca, is ready and willing to take over Bernard from Prisca. And so, the stage is set for a series of destruction and jealousies started by Bernard's initial anger. But the tool used is sex.

There are also some women who are angry at the various forms of male domination and suppression. But instead of constructing their criticism in a healthy way, they express their anger through sex by developing a style of sexual life that eliminates men. Again, sex is used as an avenue to register one's discontent of gender conflicts.

Sex used to get Infantile Love

There is a difference between love among adults and the love we feel as children in regard to our parents. Adults love each other as equals. But toward their parents, children feel small and that they are persons to be taken care of.

It frequently happens that some young men and women have intercourse with older men and women just to feel like a child with them. Friederich observes that this is common among women. The relationship between them and these 'old daddies' is that of a father and a daughter. In such a relationship "the woman's motivation is to feel attractive and accepted and protected by a parental figure. She wishes to be held and fondled much like a small child. The woman may be coquettish and sexually provocative yet 'shocked' when the man responds with a sexual advance"[11]. Usually, the relationship is established and sustained by the mutual needs of the older man and the younger woman: the man needs someone to pet as a father, and the young woman needs a father to pet her, and so, a tacit contract is entered into to take care of each other's need.

But there are also young men whose need for a caring maternal figure is obtained through sexual intercourse with an older woman. Such women generally are of high social class, with money and social standing. But these women are probably lonely and so they seek sexual pleasure with younger men. With such men these women express their motherly care and obtain their sexual needs.

Sex used as a Sign of Independence

It seems to me also that some students in the university and other institutions of higher learning engage in sexual intercourse as a demonstration of having gained their independence from their families. There are some for whom it is a symbol that they are now grown up, that no one should tell them what to do, and that they can manage their lives. It is such people who sometimes taunt their peers who are not engaging in sexual intercourse as being mommy's boy or girl, people yet to grow up. The weak ones who are unable to bear the criticism go out to prove that they are now free from their parents, and can make their own decisions. And one of such first decisions is to have sex.

Sex for Curiosity

Sometimes some people have sex in order to satisfy their curiosity, and not because they are in love. They could be teenagers or adults. They are persons who have heard about sex and what is involved in it from other people, and are unable to free themselves from the imagination of what it is like. Not satisfied with imagining, they go ahead and have sex.

Synthesis

These examples are meant to illustrate the point that sex is both attractive and ambiguous. People can engage in sex for many reasons other than for love and affection. Most importantly, these experiences show that sex itself is flexible and is never an isolated event in our lives. Our sexuality expresses our need to give and receive love, our need for wholeness, and becomes a privileged occasion to demonstrate one's inner disposition to give oneself as a gift to another. Yet, "any emotional need may find an expression through sexual activity, at times to the point where there may be very little loving or being loved involved"[12]. Herein lie the difficulties, the illusions, the hurts, and the disappointments that are encountered in many relationships: sexual activity expresses something other than love! When this happens, rather than the persons getting closer to each other in life-commitment and mutual self-disclosure, discontent, exploitation, and loneliness grow.

You can now see that sex is a complex matter that cries for understanding and integration. Perhaps your own personal experience or the experience of your friends will enable you to grasp the complexity. This discussion also offers you the opportunity to examine your desires and see how they may seek to find expression in explicit sexual acts.

At this point in our reflection, I can now confidently get into the phenomenon of love, especially the one expressed in romance, since this occupies a very significant place in the drama of human experience.

Chapter Three

Appearance and Reality in Romantic Love

The Event of Falling in Love

The phrase "to fall in love" is itself expressive of the nature and power of Eros. It is what we fall into, without consultation, as if we have been tripped by a piece of stone or stump and we fall into it, unplanned and unsuspecting. It just happens, and we feel it as an invasion. This is one way it happens to some people. Because of the suddenness of this experience, people call it infatuation or love at first sight. In other cases there is a build-up in a relationship that eventually culminates in falling in love. For instance, the persons concerned have some admiration for each other. They also tend to like being together, talking together, and telling stories. Somehow, these events prepare them for that experience of falling in love with each other. Whichever way people experience falling in love, it depends greatly on their personality and level of maturity.

When we fall in love with someone, we are falling into a deep ocean of power and strong emotions personified in and carried by the loved one who represents incredible beauty, goodness, and delight that invites us to savour and contemplate. Above all, he or she is life, joy, peace, and meaning. Henceforth everything and every person can wait, because nothing and no person matters more than the loved one. Without him or her, life would lose its meaning. It is no use going to school or studying hard if, at the end, the loved one is going to be lost. Right now, everything derives its relevance from this love.

The people who have fallen in love crave and pine for being together, and the absence of one of them is hell, an anguish that disturbs the usual flow of life. Life is no longer the same after this event. Internally the lovers are both happy and helpless in this "divine" visitation. Everything within him has become possessed by the image of the beloved: his ability to reason and follow the logic of life has fallen under this power. Before him or her, there is no hiding anymore, no pretence to be in control of one's life. One loses the desire to protect oneself in this love. "Take me with you for I am yours", they feel and say to each other.

Externally also, life is no longer totally controllable because everything starts and ends with the beloved or the lover. All previous points of reference are under threat: the rules and morals set by parents and society, the religious and moral beliefs previously held, and even personally held convictions. These are either set aside or are disorganized and reorganized by the demands of this love. It is then that the "good boy" starts to behave differently: he can lie to get away and see the beloved, and will consider it an honour for the beloved. Sometimes he caresses and fondles the beloved and cares less about the morals. The beloved on the other hand may steal some money to buy gifts for him. They are ready to please each other even if it means displeasing any other person or social institution.

Secondly, under the explosive power of Eros, all rigid structures and boundaries are altered or readjusted or even destroyed if they refuse readjustment or rearrangement[1]. It is no longer important whether he or she is an Igbo or Yoruba or Efik, Anglican or Catholic, from a rich or poor family, intelligent or not intelligent, learned or unlearned, short or tall, fat or thin, fair or black, and so on. These social categories and structures lose their sense to the lovers, and cannot be obeyed unless reorganized because such obedience ruins the infinite joy and wellbeing that this love has released in them. In this sense, every event of romantic love carries with it some seeds of disobedience to established moral, cultural, racial or religious rules. Stories of romantic love show this to be true. The Montague and the Capulet families were long-time enemies. But when Romeo, a Montague, fell in love with Juliet, a Capulet, the hate between the two families had to be faced, surmounted, and done away with or be reorganized. The struggle and the effort to reorganize this structure of hate between the two families could be seen in one of the frustrations voiced out by Juliet. In the silence of her heart, in the absence of Romeo, she cried out to him: "Deny your father. Refuse your name! Or if you will not, be my love and I'll no longer be a Capulet. It is your name that is my enemy. Oh, be some other name! What's in a name! If we call a rose by any other name it would smell as sweet. So would Romeo were he not called Romeo. Romeo, throw off your name, and take all myself!" And from the shadow of the night, Romeo responded: "Call me but love and I'll be new baptized, I will be Romeo no more"[2]. They did not succeed in breaking the walls of hate between their families in the brief period of their love, but, at their death, the two families were reconciled, and each "swore to raise a statue in pure gold in honour of the other's child; so would all know the tale of Romeo and Juliet, who fell before the venom of an ancient war, and only whose deaths had sounded the final call to peace"[3]. Eros is particularly good at this kind of thing.

When we fall in love, everything becomes different: we lose our orientation and bearing, and find ourselves in a completely new world with new language and new sight. It is like a new universe has emerged, "at the center of which are two lovers"[4]. The people around do not understand us for we have changed in our thinking, attitudes and behaviour, and we radiate a new confidence in life. But we don't even understand ourselves as well, for what is happening to us is often difficult to express. We can no longer live the way we used to without pains and suffering. We have the moral laws and social structures to fight against in as much as they guide the expression of our feelings. And how sure are we to win? Secondly, the sea of love in which we find ourselves puts us in contact with uncertainty: where is this leading? Thus love, which is a great source of joy, peace, and wellbeing, is also a source of anguish. This anguish derives from the contradictions and conflicting emotions within, and the demands that our social life makes on us as human beings. Despite the intense feelings of joy and wellbeing that love generates, the possibility that the lover or the beloved may eventually leave remains a permanent torment.

Being-in-Love: the Face of Eros in Stories

The story of Nnamdi and Ijeoma; they say they are in love. They experience intense feelings of affection and longing for each other. When they are together, the sun may stop shining because the difference between night and day is obliterated before them. Time and space are dissolved into an eternal now that is suffused in a flood of sweet feelings. Gazing at Ijeoma, Nnamdi loses words and can only contemplate this goddess of beauty and love that sits beside him. She is the perfect and ideal woman that makes him feel one with life and complete. As Ijeoma listens to his sweet words and watches his lips move, she is convinced that she has found the man of her dream.

In each other's arms, life's pains and agonies are forgotten. Life can go on or it can stand still, it does not matter provided they are together. For better or worse, nothing is better than living and dying together. Every moment that passes intensifies the longing for each other, for union, for togetherness, and the whole of life wears a new face, a new dawn, a new experience, the experience of *Eros*. Life is not very meaningful without the other; it is sour, tasteless, a drudgery, an experience permeated with intense longing for and preoccupation with the beloved. This is Eros at work.

When two persons are under the power of Eros, people often describe them as being-in-love or as having taken a love potion. Or, you do hear people say that a woman has given a man love potion and, because of that, he does not listen to his parents or friends anymore; he whines and pines for the woman. Sometimes a man will love a woman so much that people suspect she holds him captive with magic (*ọgwụ*) or charm. The suspicion is even higher if the two persons in love come from some opposing races, religion, social class, ethnic group, etc.

The best way to look at these stories is to see them as the efforts we make to understand this *thing* that is happening between persons like Nnamdi and Ijeoma. Stories like that of Nnamdi and Ijeoma and the classical myths of romantic loves try to express this *thing*, this Eros that is so powerful that when it invades people, almost from beyond space, the persons experiencing it seem unable to help themselves. The Greeks believe that erotic love comes from the abode of the gods: it is the goddess Aphrodite and her son Eros who afflict people with erotic passion so that it is experienced as a destiny. This real face of erotic love is painted so well in the classical myth of romantic love between Tristan and Queen Iseult[5].

Tristan is the son of the dead King Rivalin of Lyonesse, and Queen Blanchfleur who is the sister of King Mark of Cornwall. Fate and destiny combine together to bring Tristan to his uncle's palace. The king loves Tristan so much and intends to hand over the kingdom to him, since he has no wife or children. This fuels the anger and envy of the barons (the king's counsellors) against Tristan. As events finally turn out, under the advice of the barons, the king decides to have a wife, and it happens to be the princess of Ireland, Iseult the Fair. Tristan, a strong warrior, vows to the King to win the princess and bring her to him. He wins the princess by killing the Dragon that menaces the people of Ireland. Before Tristan and Iseult set out for Cornwall with their companions, Iseult's mother, the Queen of Ireland, "gathered herbs and flowers and roots and steeped them in wine, and brewed a portion of might", the love potion, and put it in a jar and handed it to Brangien, the princess's maid. It is the power of this potion that those who drink of it "love each other with their every single sense and with their every thought, forever, in life and in death"[6]. Iseult's mother warns Brangien to make sure that no one drinks the brew except King Mark and the princess who is now officially the Queen of Cornwall. Brangien gives her word and makes sure that things are in order.

They sail on the sea. On one sunny day, Tristan and Iseult become famished and thirsty for wine. An ignorant maid searches for something for them to drink. She finds that pitcher which contains the love potion, and hands it over to them. They drink the potion and empty the pitcher. From then on, their lives change; they are filled with joy and anguish, for their love for each other torments them. They are completely consumed with each other, with many visitations from Venus, the goddess of sexual passion. Now, how do you expect the two lovers to live when they arrive in Cornwall, and the Queen takes her position besides the King?

When they reach Cornwall, Tristan and Iseult engage in the most sophisticated intrigues and subterfuges in order to see each other and let themselves go in each other's' arms. They battle with honour and shame: the honour of their love for each other and the shame of subverting the legal marriage between the King and the Queen. They are torn between what they feel in their hearts for each other and the social and moral norms of relationship. At the time of their momentary separation Tristan tells Queen Iseult: "One day friend, we shall go together to a fortunate land from which none returns. There, rises a castle of white marble; at each of its thousand windows burns a lighted candle; at each a minstrel plays and sings a melody without end; the sun does not shine there but none regrets his light: it is the happy land of the living"[7].

Under the power of Eros, this energy of romantic love, for Tristan and Iseult, as for Nnamdi and Ijeoma, life is meaningless for one without the other. The longing and desire for union that wrenches the heart seeks for resolution, a consummation that is never satisfied by sexual passion but may even be exacerbated by that. The beloved is so unique and irreplaceable that the lovers describe themselves as soulmates, destined from eternity for each other. With the entrance of sex in love, the lovers are faced with dealing not only with the shadows of love itself but also with the ambiguity in sexual desire.

Sex and Being-in-Love

From the discussions in chapters one and two, it is clear to you that sex does not always express love. You know it from your own experience or from the experience of others. It is shown everywhere in movies, both local and foreign. You also read it in novels. Pornography that is widespread today is strictly aimed at helping people have sex as and when they want it. It says little of love. What then is the relationship between sex and the love that is generally called eros, which we have described?

In responding to this question, I draw from the ideas of C.S. Lewis in his book *The Four Loves*. Lewis uses the Greek word *Eros* in its original sense of "being in love" that happens between a man and a woman; this does not necessarily include or imply sex. The sex which human beings have in common with animals he calls Venus. This distinction has a long history, which is not our interest here. The important point this distinction brings out is that sex can operate without Eros or as part of Eros[8].

Eros represents that shattering experience of love between a man and a woman, between the lover and the beloved; it is that state in which there is the experience of suspension of everything and every person, and thoughts, imagination, fantasy, and indeed everything, is suffused with the beloved. Lewis notes that "a man in this state really hasn't leisure to think of sex. He is too busy thinking of a person. The fact that she is a woman is far less important than the fact that she is herself"[9]. When the explicitly sexual element is awakened in them, it is often not felt as having been there at the root of the relationship. It is like "Eros enters into him like an invader, taking over and reorganizing, one by one, the institutions of a conquered country. It may have taken over many others before it reaches the sex in him; and it will reorganise that too"[10]. Thus, Venus, the explicit sexual act, can exist without Eros and when it does, it wants "the *thing in itself*"[11], that is, the sexual pleasure simple and short. But Eros wants the Beloved; it contemplates her, delights in thinking about her. The focus of Eros is the person of the Beloved, the focus of Venus is the sexual pleasure.

Already from this distinction and analysis, it is obvious that there is a big difference between a person who operates mostly under the command of Venus and the one who operates under the power of Eros; it is the one under the power of Eros who is in love. Eros is qualitatively of a higher level of existence than Venus. The reason is clear: we share Venus with other animals; but in Eros, the person is conscious of the value of the *other* as a human person. But it also indicates that relationship can be lived or organized at the level of Venus, where the *utility* of the other is more important, where there is no emotional tie, as in a secondary relationship. In certain relationships that *appear* to be romantic or under the rule of Eros, it is Venus that is principally at work, leaving behind its trail, tolls of wounded and disappointed persons. In those instances, Venus mimics Eros in order to get a fill of its desire. You will already feel it within yourself, that it can be awful to relate with a person who is driven solely by Venus.

Human maturity demands that we make the first and essential step of moving from operating purely at the level of Venus to that of Eros, in which one can really be in love and give oneself over to the contemplation of the Beloved. The reason why this movement is necessary is because the heart of every person yearns for love, because we are meant to love and be loved. You saw in chapter two that people often engage in sex in order to be loved, to be valued, to be important to someone. These are the desires of *Eros*. But again, you see that most of the time, the desire and the question which emerge at the level of Eros are often settled at the level of Venus. Eros, as we shall see, gets intertwined in this problem especially when it hopes to achieve this union through sexual passion. This results in terrible disappointments, disillusion, and hurts. In some people, the experience of disappointment intensifies the search for another lover; and in others, the reaction is that of a complete closure to further relationships. In either case, the real question is yet to be raised and the true desire yet to be identified.

Illustrative Vignette

Examples of common experiences of people will help. Perhaps you can relate to them. First is the story of James and Joanne. James tells Joanne that he loves her to bits and buys things for her as a sign of his love for her. But he insists that Joanne does not love him unless they both have sex, because love between a man and woman that has no sex in it is empty and useless. Joanne, feeling indebted for the gifts received, and not wanting to lose him, goes to bed with James. As long as Joanne needs those gifts and his company and James needs to gratify his sexual desire, there is a perfect agreement: you give me A and I give you B. They are committed to each other in what *appears* to be a romantic experience, but fundamentally they are committed to gifts and sex. During holidays, James feels free to go after other young women with the same promises and demands, and Joanne, feeling unsure about her fate with James, looks out for the "right guy" with whom "to settle". As she tries out the guys for their love, she fills up her store of gifts and increases her sexual partners. But as it stands, both James and Joanne, and those like them, appear to be in a romantic relationship, but they only engage themselves in the game of mutual exploitation and deception because at the center of their relationship is the *self*, and not the other person. They exchange sweet words to each other as long as their selfish desires are met, for they have no other reason to be together. Though they appear to be in a primary relationship, they feel lonely at the depth of their being. When gifts no longer come and sex comes less frequently, the terms of their game come out clearly: they leave each other so fast and move on to others!

There is another example. In the circumstances of today, some married people find it increasingly difficult to believe that they can and should stick to each other for the rest of their lives because, as one man put it, "how can you really stay with one woman morning, afternoon, and night all the days of your life? It's just boring, impossible and difficult!" In other words, marital fidelity is impossible. Therefore, these people find alternative ways of coping with the difficulty. In Europe and North America, some believe that marital infidelity helps the marital relationship because sexual attraction between couples diminishes after some years. Therefore, the arrival of a new lover will help to rekindle the relationship[12]. Sometimes the man and the woman decide to get themselves "lovers" outside their marriage while remaining married! In many cultures, both the man and the woman in this difficulty often choose to find their own secret "lovers" (which I prefer to call "sex-providers") and meet with them in secret, just "for variety sake!" Sometimes the roles are inverted so that the legitimate husband or wife becomes the "sex provider" to the mistress or to the extramarital partner. Observe a mix up of love and sex in this example, and where the emphasis lies.

There is also another example that is typical. Anthony and Josephine are in a relationship. Josephine is happy with Anthony and desires that he marry her. Therefore, she does not refuse any request made by Anthony, especially the request to sleep with her. Apart from these intense moments of sexual union, they have nothing in common. Yet, Josephine brags that she is in love with him, and every indication shows he is going to marry her. Her girlfriends congratulate her and some are jealous. Meanwhile, Anthony goes after another girl he wants to marry and proposes to her; Josephine feels bad that she had been used and dumped. Yet, Anthony never mentioned to Josephine that their relationship was to end up in marriage. And Josephine has not asked him any day where their relationship was going. Anthony does not save a thought for Josephine; and Josephine is preoccupied with Anthony more as a husband than as a person. She is too quick to judge that her method of winning Anthony to marriage is going to work. As long as both of them have not sat down and discussed their relationship, Josephine should not accuse Anthony of being mean. At the same time, Anthony should have been able to let Josephine know the nature of their relationship. He may be relating to Josephine from the secondary level, desiring simply sex from her, and she is relating with him from the primary level, expecting a greater emotional bonding that could lead to marriage. She will definitely feel bad because she is emotionally invested in the relationship while he is not. When two persons are relating at two unequal levels, there is bound to be conflicts and hurts. Above all, when people are very much unaware of what drives them into a relationship and what they expect from it, they may burn their fingers and toes quickly and easily.

These examples illustrate that not all relationships which appear to be romantic in which *Eros* is ruling, are truly so. Again, there is no better way to be aware of this except to know your feelings and what you are looking for as well as what is driving you into a relationship with another person. But the way to get at these feelings is to communicate with each other. We live in a culture where people are not encouraged to put in words the way they feel in love relationships for fear they might be misunderstood. Honest verbalization of one's state could have prevented certain disasters among people who are in love. Sometimes, it is even painful for married people to say the way they feel to each other. The ability to communicate well what one is going through is an integral part of any true love relationship.

Chapter Four

Does He Love me, Does She Love me: Truly?

How many men and women, young and old, ask this question every day? On those occasions that I had the opportunity to speak to some young people it was one of the recurring questions. The fact that we raise these questions at all implies that everything is not smooth in romantic love. It is a common experience that many men have dumped the women they said they loved before and a good number of women have also abandoned their love in pursuit of other men. What starts off as a true experience of romantic love can end up in serious hate. You have heard stories of a man and a woman who were in love for many years, and at the end, the man leaves the woman and goes after another whom he takes to the altar for marriage. And three years into the marriage, he leaves the wife for another woman, perhaps a younger one. The story can be the other way round: a woman leaves her boyfriend of many years and goes with another she may feel is stronger and with more financial status.

These are the experiences that lead to seething anger and hate that, in some cases, end up in destruction of persons and properties. Or, it can hurt so deeply that the persons affected are unable to come out of it for the rest of their lives. These things happen in movies and you read about them in novels. They are sources of concern and worry to people who say they are in love; it is like you are not quite sure. Yet, people cannot stop falling in love; it is something that happens always.

In order to give a personal response to the question of whether he or she truly loves you, there are aspects of romantic love itself that you should be aware of. I wish to present two of them here: the tragic element that is present in romantic love and the possibility that the beloved can be dumped when the passion fades.

The Tragic Element in Romantic Love

The experience of Eros is an overwhelming experience. Henceforth everything derives and leads to it. Nothing on earth can prevent the lovers from "worshipping" each other in this well of life, peace, joy, and union. Everything else is secondary, and all life is subject to the dynamics of this experience. You may have heard of young people who, under the spell of Eros, have bound themselves forever through licking their blood or taking vows that nothing will separate them from each other. Eros can do such things.

Eros is limited and excruciating in its demands: it imposes upon this particular individual and this particular relationship to provide satisfaction for this longing for "a forever", a union that knows no mutation, no change, a union that lasts forever and ever; a life of bliss that does not wane. There is simply nothing bad or abnormal that lovers yearn for greater and deeper bonding or intimacy. But it does not have to be a genital bonding. When lovers are largely immature, it is very easy for them to seek this union through sex. The greater the immaturity, the more sex becomes the available means of entering into that unknown world of union where the lovers will be bound to each other forever without separation. The persistent demand of Eros for union of the lovers and the search for this union in sex is the reason why erotic love has earned the name of "Carnal Love". In actual fact, though the desire for union makes erotic love tend to dwell on the body, the driving force is not sex; it is union with the beloved, the permanent possession of her or him. While the desire for union with the beloved is a good thing, it can constitute a serious problem when the lovers are inclined to seek this union in sex because of immaturity and ignorance. Now, see why this is so.

The more the lovers meet together and sincerely seek this *eternal union* through sexual passion, the realization of their separateness at the end is more

LOVE: WITH OR WITHOUT SEX?

frustrating. After each fill of sexual passion, they come back to themselves and realize the inability of sex to bind them together. The sexual expression promises to be the bridge that will bring them to the other side of life where their togetherness and the bliss that comes from it will remain permanent. But this end is unattainable in this life. The desire of love is beyond this world, and those who are reasonably mature realize this. Immature persons struggle to realize it here in this world, and this may simply end up in sex which does not "produce the substantial unit that I crave"[1]. This is why there is too much pain and grief in romantic love; it cannot really provide that which it seems to promise: a happiness that endures onto eternity. This pain is experienced by everyone in love. Those who are mature or are growing to maturity acknowledge it and place it within the limits of our humanity. The immature ones are carried away by this longing and get more frustrated in trying to achieve it in sex. C.S. Lewis describes the situation well: "the longing for a union which only the flesh can mediate while the flesh, our mutually excluding bodies, renders it forever unattainable can have the grandeur of a metaphysical pursuit. Amorousness as well as grief can bring tears to the eyes"[2]. But Eros is so overpowering in its inspiration and sweet in its sounds that ears are deaf to other voices contrary to its burning desire to possess and unite with the

Beloved. For in her or in him, it appears, perfect happiness will be found.

When people who are in love are largely immature such as when they feel deeply insecure in themselves, empty, unloved and unhappy, then Eros can be invested with this project of providing perfect security and perfect happiness. It is then that tragedy is around the corner. In that state, the erotic desires of the lovers can prescribe lawlessness in the name of love: "the love which leads to cruel and perjured unions, even to suicide-pacts and murder, is not likely to be wandering lust or idle sentiment. It may well be Eros in all his splendour; heart-breakingly sincere; ready for every sacrifice except renunciation"[3]. It introduces its own moral law: only that which pleases the beloved is of value! This can sanction infidelity and deceit. The intrigues and infidelities of the lovers are often experienced "as thrust upon them by something more holy than the laws that they violate. For their love has made them one, and this unity of two beings excuses every ruse toward a world that would divide them"[4].

It is here that the tragedy lies: when the immature conditions of lovers are projected onto Eros and are honoured and obeyed unconditionally, then Eros turns into a demon. "Divinely indifferent to our selfishness, he is also demonaically rebellious to every claim of God or Man that would oppose Him"[5]. Hence most of the time, immature persons in romantic love could give up even their education, their cherished dreams and legitimate relationships and follow after the god of Eros fashioned according to their image. Sometimes, it ends up in tragedy, at other times, it leaves countless atrocities in its path: illegitimate children, immature decisions, and a life of sourness and regrets.

But Eros is not really the problem. It must not be rejected nor its power underrated. It is most sincere in its actions. Eros that finds expression in sexual passion is not the pure Venus, which wants just sex and nothing more. Eros seeks union with the beloved, and not simply the gratification of concupiscent desires. Eros is the strongest experience of love a human being undergoes, such that C.S. Lewis calls it the "King of all pleasures". Pleasure here does not mean the pleasure of sex but that pleasure or sweetness of friendship, of loving, of being together, and of mutual self-giving. Eros is god-like in quality and has a feeling of eternity as it courses through the blood of the lovers. Despite the destruction it can leave in its path depending on our level of affective maturity, it is the love that resembles God who is love Himself[6]. People who are touched by the love of God will almost feel the same rapture that is close to the experience of romantic love. That is why contemplatives understand the dynamics of romantic love so well because it reflects, as a matter of resemblance, their own relationship with God.

The other side of this tragedy is the menace of possessiveness in erotic love. Though the lover is focused on the beloved, and wants the beloved, the desire for union does not allow the romantic lover to see and appreciate the *apartness* or the separateness of the beloved; his desire for her does not give him the space to consider her interests, and all she wants is to possess and have him to herself, completely and totally, to the exclusion of others. The more immature the lovers are, the greater the intensity of this possessiveness and the fear of losing the beloved or the lover. Trust is difficult to build in such a relationship because of personal insecurity and other conflicts. When this is the case romantic love is fuelled by intense self-interest that fears the autonomy of the *other*. Both the lover and the beloved view each other from the intense perspective of their desire for complete attachment. Because of this tendency, the romantic lovers experience little freedom: they seek to possess and hold each other, and this becomes a significant source of distress and anxiety. The result is that romantic love is experienced as a kind of oppression, a kind of closeness to each other that closes in on the persons to the point of suffocation and death. For Scruton, this is the fundamental reason why romantic lovers are usually eaten up by jealousy, war, envy and guardedness[7]. But the problem does not lie in Eros itself but in the immaturity of romantic lovers.

As you can see, if romantic lovers do not grow to maturity, Eros can destroy them. The suffocation of possessiveness can set the stage for the struggle for freedom which may lead to the point of destructiveness when the lover loses consciousness of the beloved's uniqueness.

The Beloved can be dumped

This is another problem that is made worse by our immaturity. In erotic or romantic love, it is the person who is valued as an individual. The beloved is the object of the lover's thoughts and feelings. She is unique, not like any other, and the lover focuses on her. Now these thoughts and feelings which dwell on the beloved can be sustained if "the lover maintains his beloved's status in his feelings as a unique person, the sole recipient and object of his passion, raised above the *generalizing transactions of the body*"[8]. In other words, if the lover is not able to rise above the "generalizing transactions of the body" perhaps due to his immaturity, low self-esteem, feelings of emptiness that, he can allow his thoughts and feelings to dwell on other "bodies" so that the beloved loses her place in his feelings and thoughts, and may no longer be the sole recipient of his passion. This implies that the fire of Eros directed to the beloved is now burning less and less. This makes some people start to look for other persons who can excite them sexually. And this is where the generalizing tendency of the body takes over and leads to the loss of the beloved. How does it happen?

The "generalizing transactions of the body" means the ability of the body to respond to different forms of sexual appeal. You know that you can be excited sexually by some persons, or even by pornography. In this manner, the body can generalize its desire for sexual gratification. When this generalizing transaction of the body dominates the consciousness of the lover and gives direction to romantic love, then the beloved may lose her uniqueness and becomes any kind of individual, replaceable, transferable, and even universal[9]; then sexual passion can migrate freely from one person to another as if to indicate that every girl is a female and every boy is a male. It is true that every girl is a female and every boy a male, but not every girl is *the* beloved, and not every boy is *the* lover. This is the difference. As long as every girl is a female and every boy a male, sexual passion is set free to relate to the universal male or female available to satisfy it rather than to persons or individuals, which is what romantic love seeks. But here the desires of Eros have been transposed into the desire for pure sex. This transposition is carried out not by Eros but by the immature persons in the relationship.

To illustrate this issue, let us take the example of what happens between the prostitute and her client. From the start of the transaction, both the prostitute and her client, though individuals, are veiled from their subjective uniqueness. In this veil, there is some form of internal detachment from their consciousness of being unique individuals, so that all attention is directed to the sexual act and the pleasure it gives. It is the same thing that happens in all forms of obscenity, perversion, paedophilia, and others. In these instances, it is not the individual, the unique individual, which is desired, but the act which is performed with him or her[10]. What should become a commitment between persons guarded and protected by the discipline of chastity "becomes a sensation in the private parts. The sexual sacrament gives way to a sexual market; and the result is ... a fetishism of the sexual commodity: in other words, a fundamental displacement of interest from the individual to the generality of his or her sex"[11]. At this point the gradual transposition of the desires of Eros into the explicit sex has been completed and the immature lovers are confirmed in their immaturity unless they realize their need to grow.

In the light of this, Scruton distinguishes between the *caress of affection* and the *caress of desire*. The caress of affection, the caress of love, the caress of Eros, is the caress of the beloved, and it is "a gesture of reassurance"[12] in which the lover attempts to place in the beloved's consciousness his concern and care for her. It is the caress that recognizes the validity of the beloved, her irreplaceability. This caress goes back to that human touch that we experienced as children from our parents and significant others. It is that touch that assures us that we are important and that we can have faith in life and in the world. When Jesus touches people in this way, he brings God's love and healing to their lives.

The caress of desire, on the other hand, is the caress of Venus, of the sexual act which "merely *outlines* the body of the recipient; it is an exploratory rather than a reassuring gesture"[13], and in it the uniqueness of the individual is lost. It can be directed to any person as long as he or she possesses a body to be outlined. This is why in all sexual perversions and obscenities, the flesh, the body, that object of interest "is represented in such a way as to become opaque to the self that inhabits it"[14].

The veil of the "sexual object" covers the consciousness of the subjective self which is unique, so that the persons can relate sexually without a deeper involvement that goes beyond the body. Whenever the opaqueness lifts and the individual is aware of him or herself, guilt follows, not simply the guilt of having offended God, but an existential guilt that one has violated oneself. That is to say, that one has lost his or her uniqueness in the non-specificity of maleness and femaleness. And this is why the person feels revulsion toward the person who is presumed to have carried out the act of violation.

You can see how easy it is for the lover to dump the beloved, and how the process works to lead to that event that leaves indelible wounds in the heart. And if you add this reality to the ambiguity of sex which we presented in chapter two, then it will be easy for you to see why there will be pain and agony in love relationships especially when the lovers have not attained a reasonable degree of affective maturity.

But there is a question yet to be addressed: why is it that the lover may not be able to rise above the generalizing transactions of the body? It is simply because the fire of romantic passion does diminish in its intensity and may fade. When this happens and the lovers are not aware of it, they may wake up one day and find out that they have lost that intense pull to each other. This may bring a set of new attitudes that may lead them to transformation if they are growing or to deeper problems if they are stuck in their immaturity and are unable to understand what is happening to them and talk about it.

When the Romantic Passion fades

I return to the story of Tristan and Iseult to illustrate my point. They are still under the spell of romantic love and allow their sexual passions to flow freely as they seek for this union. They escape to the Wood of Morois where they stay and live on the flesh of wild animals. They suffer so much deprivation that they lose weight and their clothes are torn by the briars. But they love each other so much that they do not know they are suffering. One day, as they are in the woods, a hermit, Ogrin by name, a holy man, meets the two of them and speaks to Tristan in these words: "God aid you, Lord Tristan; for you have lost both this world and the next! A man that is traitor to his lord is worthy to be torn by horses and burnt upon the faggot, and wherever his ashes fall no grass shall grow and all tillage is waste, and the trees and the green things die. Lord Tristan, give back the Queen to the man who espoused her lawfully according to the laws of Rome…. Do penance, Tristan! God pardons the sinner who turns to repentance"[15]. And Tristan replies: "And of what should I repent, Ogrin, my Lord? Or of what crime? You that sit in judgment upon us here, do you know what cup it was we drank upon the high sea? That good, great draught inebriates us both. I would rather beg my life long and live off roots and herbs with Iseult than, lacking her, be king of a wide kingdom"[16].

If Nnamdi were confronted in the same way, he would reply in the same manner saying that he knew what he was doing, that he was in love, and that he would not exchange Ijeoma for anything. That is why people are surprised when, after some time, he begins to disregard Ijeoma and goes after other girls, or vice versa. People interpret it as dishonesty on his part and call him a womanizer, and Ijeoma is described as a wayward woman. But the situation is deeper than that. Romantic love is experienced by individuals who are members of a vast society of human beings. When romantic lovers walk head-on against these social norms that protect stable relationships, it can bring some troubles to them. Iseult was the first who realized that when she said that they should go back to the King where she belonged and ask for mercy and forgiveness from God[17]. They did not catch that moment of enlightenment, and eventually they died.

The tragic end of most myths and stories of romantic love is metaphoric: it reflects the inability of romantic lovers to accept the limitations imposed on us by our being human. The lovers entertain the desire to see the finitude of their separate bodies, of life on earth, and the norms of social life, vanish from before them so that their life will be an endless communion of one with the other. It is thus that their devotion to each other turns into a kind of affliction and obsession especially if they are very immature. But if we are sufficiently secured in ourselves, we will not fall into the trap of mourning our finitude and limitations. We accept them and work with and through them towards greater personal growth and integration.

The tendency of some lovers to dwell on sex in search of this union usually produces its own morality, the morality of sexual passion. In this "new morality", devotion to the beloved and sex is of primary importance; nothing is thought to have the power to stop it. The lovers put aside every value and rule in order to seek the ecstasy, rapture and mind-searing experience that makes them feel on top of the world. The force of passion derives mostly from the needs of our personality. And, depending on the level of affective maturity, the passion can be so strong that some say it is inhuman not to allow its expression. But the passion often fades, and when it does, it simply "migrates to someone else we feel attracted to. If we are committed only to follow where passion leads, then there can be no true loyalty to an individual person"[18]. How is it that after sometime, Nnamdi will lose interest in the Ijeoma he had adored before and is now going after Nkiru?

It is not difficult to see how we can do that if we are not mature enough. This is what happens. You remember that when romantic lovers engage in sex, it is not the sex as such that they are looking for, but an enduring bonding or union. But at the end of each act, the lovers experience the fact that this eternal bliss of permanent union is an illusion. Before you know it, the passion of sex starts to wane, and this is made worse by the experience of possessive suffocation. Then the lovers begin to see themselves truly as they are in their real beauty and ugliness. Disappointment is the result. Those men and women, who cannot face this disappointment can easily get attracted to another person so that a vicious cycle is created: the passion of sex lifts from one person and rests on another.

You can see that with the passage of time, the immature romantic lover may become less and less loyal to an individual and more and more to the passion of sex. And without loyalty to the individual person in his or her beauty and ugliness, gifts and limits, and as belonging to a society with rules and customs, it is difficult to experience and maintain true love and a fulfilling relationship. This is the ultimate tragedy of immaturity in a love relationship and Iseult expresses it well: she does not truly love Tristan and neither does he love her.

It does not literally mean they don't love each other; it rather suggests they are unable to rise beyond their passion for each other and for sex. If they could, then Iseult would have gone back to the King's palace where she belonged, while still maintaining a friendship with Tristan. And Tristan himself would have been able to accept the fact that he was not going to live with Iseult the Fair as husband and wife. Loyalty to the passion attached to Iseult the Fair could not allow him to develop the more realistic relationship with Iseult of White Hands with whom he could have had a life of husband and wife. In both cases, the fog of passion made denser by immaturity prevents a grounding in the reality of real persons. The conclusion is the death of Tristan and Iseult the Fair.

This tale shows the need for us to grow as persons and develop that capacity to love in a reasonable way. Even in such intense moment of love, there is still some reservoir of thoughtfulness to clarify the situation in the light of life as a whole. This is a real challenge of maturity which each of us must face. There are two passions present in that particular moment of intense feeling of love: the passion to give oneself *and* the passion to be with the beloved, the passion to develop oneself fully *and* the passion to hang on the beloved for the meaning of one's life. These two passions coexist. As we grow in maturity, the passion to make gift of ourselves and develop fully dominates and gives direction to the passion to be with the beloved permanently. If we are very immature, the passion to hang our life on the beloved will predominate because she is the source of self-esteem and self-enhancement. This is why such relationships are usually fraught with many troubles, and they tend to end in tragedy.

Does He/She love Me then?

To the question, then, as to whether he or she truly loves you, the response demands serious attention to the feelings and motives that the two of you experience. But above all, it depends on the level of personal maturity two of you have attained and your readiness to grow together. This means that you have to know what you feel toward him, and he has to know what he feels toward you. But most importantly, you have to come to terms with the problems of romantic love, the illusions it can generate because of our various needs and conflicts, and the tendency it has to drive people to do crazy things. It is a wonderful experience, and a unique one that brings us to a very deep level of our humanity. But if we do not appreciate the challenges it poses to our growth to maturity, it can demand a union that is not possible on earth and leads to a form of attachment that can sometimes oppress more than it liberates. It becomes so centered on the self that it can impede any expansion of the heart to a bigger and more self-giving love. That is, it can forestall any further development of the individuals involved. Finally, the pleasures of sex can fade and migrate to another person.

These problems do not indicate that romantic love is a bad thing; not at all! It is a beautiful human experience. But like everything that is human, it is beset with ambiguities. The ambiguities do not lie in Eros itself but in us human beings. That is why we need to understand ourselves well and understand the message of Eros. This understanding is achieved through communication. No matter the intensity of romantic love, the persons in it should spare themselves the time to talk to each other, and say what they feel. They should be aware of their preoccupations and fears, and should be able to verbalize what they are looking for in the relationship. You know that sex is not necessarily a sign of love because it can exist with or without love. And the more your friends insist that sex should be there, the more you should question it. But this has to be done in a gentle way, because our sexual desires are generally mixed with our feelings of love. Empathy with your friend's feelings and desires is very helpful because it has the ability to lead him or her to some degree of freedom and space which are needed to examine one's feelings. But over and above all, erotic love and lovers needs some transformation.

Romantic Love and Lovers need Transformation

We can never eliminate all the problems of love, sex and relationship, for that will mean the total annihilation of human beings. But we can reduce the wounds and hurts and disappointments in ourselves and in others if we face up the challenges of our own development. This is the reason why this knowledge is worth having. Secondly, you know that we all seek love, to love and be loved, a love in which we can give ourselves totally to and receive from another in freedom; a love that is consumed with devotion to the other, a devotion that is characterized by the forgetfulness of the self. Romantic love seeks to devote itself to the beloved. But, as we saw earlier, we may be inclined to become so caught up in the intensity of our need that Eros can destroy both the lover and the beloved. When left in this condition of human immaturity, it would appear that romantic love is a venture, "without any worldly benefits or gains beyond itself"[19].

But Eros is closest to God because "it is an image, a foretaste, of what we must become to all if Love Himself rules in us without a rival. It is even a preparation for that"[20]. However, it must never be deified; it cannot be asked to give what it does not have the power to give: perfect love and perfect happiness. No one asks a two-year-old child to solve an algebraic problem. As we grow in maturity and in love relationship, we experience the pull beyond Eros toward the love that is not merely erotic; a love so deep which the human heart craves; that yearning for a "forever" experience in the arms of the beloved when the contradictions and the seemingly meaningless events and situations in life are somehow settled and everything falls into place; that yearning for life that promises to bring to an end the restlessness and agitations of the human heart; a yearning for a deeper grasp of the injustices, pains, apparent inequality in life, and the ultimate meaning of all we are and do. This is the fundamental yearning of the human heart, and it is a yearning for love. Under the weight of our human immaturities, Erotic or romantic love in its intense power and need drowns these questions and presents the Beloved as the carrier of the eternal promise.

Left to the judgment of our immaturity, Eros can be reckless and destructive as much as it can be exhilarating in the experience it provides. In order to keep to itself and remain the King of all pleasures and a preparation for our experience of union with God, Erotic lovers must challenge themselves to grow to maturity. Their growth also implies that Eros undergoes some transformation. Lewis puts it beautifully: "the god dies or becomes a demon unless he obeys God"[21]. Removed from the eye of God and fed by the ambiguities of our human nature, Eros can wreck disaster. But if it remains subject to God and we grow in our humanity, it retains its god-like quality, and does not claim to be the God. Understanding what this implies is our task in the second part of this book.

Part II

*The Transformation of Romantic Lovers
and their Love*

Chapter Five

Love Struggles with the Weaknesses of Human Nature

Love is a journey of learning. In and through it we come to know ourselves. We discover the hidden potentialities for good and for ill in ourselves. Above all, we encounter the other. And, hopefully, we make the journey together towards greater self-awareness and openness. We try to become gifts to each other and to the persons we encounter. But, out of human weaknesses, this journey can be truncated or forestalled. But the good news is that the grace of God triumphs enabling us to face the challenges of our growth amidst our brokenness, immaturities, and resistances. It is important to have this in mind as we examine the significant changes that romantic lovers and romantic love need to go through.

A starting point for a deeper appreciation of the transformation that Eros and romantic lovers need is the recognition of our predicament as human beings and the struggles of love with human weaknesses that derive from this predicament. This struggle has many faces but it is rooted in the fact that we are embodied spirits, so that we can express ourselves through our bodies, but we are not simply bodies. That is, we human beings do not just possess consciousness, but we are conscious of ourselves. We not only are aware that we are doing something, but we are also aware of our awareness. I do not only know that I am writing this book, but I am conscious of my consciousness of writing. This is what makes us persons and individuals, capable of free choice and decisions. In our Christian language, this is what it means that we are created in the image of God: that we are persons, self-conscious because God is a trinity of persons, with perfect and absolute self-consciousness. Because we are persons with "self" we can enter into a dialogue of love with each other and with God, and are capable of giving ourselves to another in love as God gave himself to us in His Christ. But our self-consciousness, our spirit, is embodied, and as bodies, we are also under the laws that rule bodies.

A second aspect of our embodiment is the fact that we do not always get everything together in our lives; it is always a struggle we engage in as long as we are alive. Most of the time, we do exactly those things we do not want to do. For this reason, we can even hurt those we love most without intending to. In other words, our embodiment is not a smooth sail through life; it can be a source of distress and anxiety. This experience of our inability to get everything together in our lives is what we call the effects of original sin, and our sexuality, our love and relationships, are the prevalent places where these effects of our wounded humanity manifest themselves.

We need to be aware of these things in our human nature in order to understand the dilemma that romantic love poses for lovers, and why and how love and lovers need to go through the process of transformation. We shall now examine the specific manifestations of this human predicament and how they are expressed in the struggles of romantic lovers.

Love and Sex: Me and My Body

If we can summarize in one sentence the tensions and problems between love and sex, especially evident in erotic love, it is this: it is the problem of understanding and managing well our embodiment; the fact that though we have a body, we are not simply a body; we are also a spirit. What do I mean by this and what is the problem?

Now, our bodies, because they follow the laws of biology, can be objectified; that is, they are objects that follow certain determined laws which we discover and study, as when we study our digestive and reproductive systems. When we do this, we are recognizing the fact that our body is an object out there, available for scientific study and analysis.

But you also realize that though you have a body that obeys the laws of biological nature, your body is also you, a person conscious of him or herself, and a person who can express him or herself freely through the body; a person who makes decisions and carries out certain actions whose direction and purpose cannot be reduced to or explained by the biological laws that determine the body. This is what we mean when we say that you are a human person, a subject who can, at the same time, be objectified.

You notice then that your sexual desire may follow the biological laws of attraction, tension, and release, but because you are a human being, you give it direction and purpose. When your female dog or goat is in sexual heat, it seeks a male to mate; it does not think about what will happen to it in the course of that or what the male will think of it. On the other hand, human beings feel violated when someone wants them just for sex. Observe also that because you are hungry does not mean you eat anything you see; you consider health risks, weight, and so on. Animals don't stop eating a thing because they care about their health or weight or how they will look, but, perhaps, because they are full or the food is not the kind they are used to. Yet, some people are under the mistaken idea that sexual desire is like hunger or thirst. Consider Freud's description of sexual desire as the "union of the genitals in the act known as copulation, which leads to a release of the sexual tension and a temporary extinction of the sexual instinct – a satisfaction analogous to the sating of hunger"[1]. This simply describes the *biological* structure of sexual desire in both human beings and beasts. But in the human being, the sexual desire does not merely follow this homeostatic rhythm Freud describes. Some people tend to think like Freud that sex is natural and should be left to be so. What they often forget is that "what is called natural for man as man is not at all the same as what the term 'natural' signifies in the case of animals; instead, conformity is natural when it is conformity to *one's own* type ..."[2]. It is not typical for cars to run in the air but typical for airplanes to do so. But both of them are means of transport. In the same way, though sexual desire and sexual intercourse in human beings and in animals have the same biological structure and lead to reproduction of species, there is an essential difference. In human beings sexual desire is "both an attraction between objects and a dialogue of subjects"[3]. This dialogue of subjects is what is expressed in love. Though sexual desire is an attraction that carries some sensations that are evident in the body, it is the desire of the whole person, body and spirit, so that it is an attraction *and* a dialogue and not either one or the other. But this also means that the dialogue of subjects, expressed in love, can be left out so that the body, as that privileged place of the sexual act, can be related to as simply object.

And this is where the predicament becomes very real and concrete, and love has to struggle with it. Because sexual desire can be objectified in the body, it can follow the determination of biological laws and run its course with little or no reference to the person. In every love, the beloved is unique, irreplaceable and without substitute; the beloved is valued as a person and true dialogue can exist between lovers. And the contact of the bodies, the caress, the kiss, are efforts to capture and relate to the mystery of the person, whole and entire. But when sex is pursued as mere object, putting aside the dialogue of persons as subjects, when someone just wants to have sex with you and is less concerned about you as a person except as one who provides sexual gratification, then "love" can accept substitutes, other sex providers. This, for Scruton, is the greatest crime against love "for by this means we leave the world of value and enter the world of price"[4]. The world of price is the world of market, of buying and selling the commodity of sex. And in this case, any seller can serve any buyer; anyone can substitute another.

Substitute 'lovers' are available to each other but they are opaque, veiled from their inner self so that in that contact of sex, there is more a meeting of bodies than of persons; there is not that encounter that opens up to self-revelation, deeper connection, and trust. In romantic love, the lover and the beloved can no longer hide behind the shells of their self-protection; the force of Eros shatters it and draws them to a real encounter one with another in which they are bound to reveal themselves and bow down before their vulnerabilities[5]. But when passion fades and erotic love degenerates into a fixation of the body and the gratification it provides, the formerly valued beloved also risks losing the awareness of her body in the consciousness of her lover because the lover may be more interested in another body; the beloved may not be desired again because she appears no longer fascinating; then it becomes easy to substitute her body, the "sexual object", with another so that true encounter at the deep level of the self becomes difficult. At this moment in relationship, encounter and communication at a deeper level between the beloved and the lover diminishes or even becomes impossible. Personal stories become more and more superficial and formal. The desire for self-protection re-emerges as a last attempt to secure the areas of one's life that have not been exposed.

There can be no true love relationship without self-disclosure, of which our nakedness is only but a symbol. Those who truly love each other know that they are naked before each other even when they are well-clothed. It is this self-disclosure, this revelation of our fears, our weaknesses, and our fragilities, that make a love relationship a real adventure in personal growth. It is this "psychic communication", this "meeting of souls"[6], that is the essence of the intimacy experienced in a love relationship.

But substitute lovers do not take such risks; "sexual bodies" don't really embarrass us nor do they seek to resist our sexual cravings[7]. They are not afraid of being abandoned after self-disclosure because the self has not been revealed at all; nothing really personal has been sacrificed for the relationship. The substitute lover can have as many partners as he or she may want for sexual variety. It is a need because when there is no deeper dialogue, the fascination of one body can be lost easily. The beloved can only be one and not two because she alone has been able to penetrate the deepest psychic world of the lover as no other person has done. The love that bonds her to the lover is the one before which the two of them stand face to face in a kind of nakedness that goes through the dense body to the hidden areas of the soul. That is why the beloved and the lover are unique and irreplaceable.

You now see why people who have sexual partners may find it difficult to give or receive love in a fulfilling relationship. The man or woman who deals with substitutes that replace one another as sexual objects can so easily develop the habit in which he or she creates "a compliant fantasy world of desire, in which unreal objects become the focus of real emotions and the emotions themselves are withdrawn from personal relations, thus impoverishing our social experience"[8]. Going down this road fundamentally alters and denigrates the "self", substituting the sex we share with animals for that complete human nature that includes the soul.

This potentiality for sex to run its course, and therefore mimic and bastardize love, is a permanent possibility in love relationship. Romantic lovers struggle with it all the time. And, according to Scruton, this explains why almost all cultures in the world place so much emphasis on chastity and sexual purity so as to help individuals integrate their sexual impulses into their personality; so that sexual desire can go "hand in hand with respect and admiration and so form the basis of a lasting union"[9]. Sexual morality aims at safeguarding all of us as embodied subjects because "at any moment we can become 'mere body,' the self-driven from its incarnation and its habitation sacked"[10]. These mores do not forbid desire; on the contrary they try to reconstitute our sexual desires as expressing our feelings of love and relationship. In doing this, sexual morality takes sexual desire from the purely physical world of objects and places it in the embodied world of our humanity so that it both expresses "attraction and love".

Substitute love occurs when you relate to my body instead of me as a person. Many a romantic love has ended up here leaving behind persons with broken-hearts and anger. It is the agony of Tereza in Milan Kundera's novel, *The Unbearable*

Lightness of Being. She had run away from her aggressive mother. Her mother had rebelled against her own failing beauty by exhibiting a kind of immodesty that makes "all bodies equal and the same". For this reason, Tereza came to Tomas, her first love, "to make her body unique, irreplaceable". They got married. But his infidelity, his prostitution with substitute lovers, has made Tereza equal to all other women: "he kissed them all alike, stroked them alike, made no, absolutely no distinction between Tereza's body and the other bodies. He had sent her back into the world she tried to escape, sent her to march naked with the other naked women"[11]. She has lost her uniqueness before him. The dialogue of unique persons had been drowned in the sea of bodies. She struggled constantly to deal with her experience of being treated as a "soulless body", a body uninhabited by a person. She came to the point where she tried to accept the fact that she might be fighting a lost war against Tomas's infidelity. Maybe, after all, her body was not unique; maybe she was taking the matter too seriously, for Tomas had told her many times that his freedom to have sex with "other bodies" was perfectly in agreement and not contradictory to his loving her, for the two are not the same![12] Then one day, she tried out a stranger, an engineer, in his apartment. When the engineer's hand started tracing her body, she had no anxiety, no fear; she stood still, motionless "for the engineer's hand referred to her body, and she realized that she (her soul) was not at all involved, only her body, her body alone. The body that had betrayed her and that she had sent out into the world among other bodies"[13]. But the "play" could not last, for she knew she was not a mere body. She could not pretend her body was not Tereza. It was her. The awareness invaded her consciousness. Then, "peering into the engineer's face, she realized that she would never allow her body, on which her soul had left its mark, to take pleasure in the embrace of someone she neither knew nor wished to know. She was filled with an intoxicating hatred. She collected a gob of saliva to spit in the stranger's face. She thrashed in his arms, swung her fists in the air, and spat in his face"[14]. But the struggle was not yet over!

The possibility of obsession with "bodies" to the loss of the uniqueness of the beloved is real given the ambiguities of human nature which we carry in ourselves. It will always be there as a potential place for the transformation of the lovers or their destruction. Without some empowerment from beyond it, Eros can easily gravitate to the pure object of sexual desire, and seek true love and relationship in substitute loves.

Baptism by Fire: the Wounds of Love

The greatest and long-lasting wounds we ever suffer come from our love relationships. The wounds of love are felt from the depth of the soul because it is in love that the individual has dared to expose himself or herself in order to unite more with the loved one. Secondly, the love relationship is felt as the strongest security against the ravages of life; any kind of pain and deprivation can be borne in love. But when love inflicts its wounds, this security is lifted, and we are left alone.

There are two moments in love relationship when love inflicts its wounds. The first is when the realization comes that the lover or the beloved is different, that he or she can't really fulfil my expectations, that he or she is not really what I had thought. The second place where love can wound is in the event of betrayal and abandonment. These wounds are always permanent possibilities in love because of our predicament as human beings. Romantic love has to deal with them.

Oh My God! He/She is not what I had thought: "Falling out of Love"

We can discover a kind of cycle in romantic relationships. There is a time of intense affection, followed by some moments of disillusionment, and then a rediscovery of oneself and the other in relationship. These three moments do not happen in a stage-like manner. They can alternate from time to time. How they happen and the outcome generally depend on the level of maturity of the persons involved. The phrase "falling out of love" expresses that second moment of disillusionment and the possible consequences.

An aspect of our human predicament in love is the reality that we are not really complete as persons, and may never achieve complete wholeness in this life. This is proved by the fact that we fall in love at all and experience the wellbeing that feels like completeness that we did not know before[15]. Or as Giddens puts it: "The other, by being who he or she is, answers a lack which the individual does not even necessarily recognize – until the love relation is initiated. And this lack is directly to do with self-identity: in some sense, the flawed individual is made whole"[16]. This goes back to show the openness of every individual to growth and the importance of relationship for this growth.

We constantly feel we lack something. Just as our embodiment places on us the burden of resisting the temptation of assuming that we are 'mere bodies', so our experience of love exposes us to the most fatal wound of the human spirit: the realization that the beloved is not what she was expected to be and that the lover is ambivalent; that we may have, after all, deluded ourselves. In falling in love, I see this person, this beloved, this lover, as the one who will be able to take care of the unhappiness in my life; my pains and sorrows shall be taken away for he or she cares for me. He or she truly understands me. In that experience of fullness, of being alive in the arms of the lover or the beloved, we hope and expect that all previous experiences of loneliness are taken away, forever. At last, I have found someone before whom I can be myself, unguarded and unprotected; someone who makes me live. In that experience the beloved or the lover represents for me stability, permanence, and invincibility in the face of life's troubles and challenges. Hence, there exists the intense desire to have the beloved always around, and the fear of losing or separating from him or her.

These expectations are true and life-giving. Indeed, "love makes life intense and meaningful", such that "when we perceive great change in another, it is less likely due to intellectual growth than to a love experience that has given a new shape to his or her life"[17]. It is the most powerful life-changing experience. But precisely because of its power to effect a vast array of changes in a person, romantic love has also the greatest power to inflict serious wounds in our lives especially if our immaturity is great.

The expectations and the dreams we have about our beloved or lover usually confront the reality of the world. It may well happen that the beloved and the lover are unable to fulfil our expectations. After some time, the lover begins to discover that the beloved can be fickle sometimes; she is not always available emotionally; she gets into moods; she loses the glow of the initial period and is unable to motivate him in life. In addition to these, she talks to and yells at him more now than before. He can't believe this was the girl he met some years back; she seems different now, irritated and irritable. She has her complaints also: he is not sensitive to her moods; he is not there for her most of the time; his business takes the better part of him; he does not talk to her enough; and she doesn't understand why he is mad at her often. Then she feels and thinks within herself "I have been deceived; he is not what he appeared to be; there must be a woman somewhere who is taking his time and attention". The dream of a wonderful woman or man is being questioned. Is she really that woman? Is he really that man? The idea of perfect man and perfect woman personified in the idealized images of the lover and the beloved is falling apart. Then, gradually, they fall out of love. The intensity of their feelings for each other has diminished. The lovers are undergoing baptism by fire, the wound that love always inflicts on the lovers to bring them to the awareness of themselves in order to lead them to transformation. This is a trying moment that holds out promise of life but also of death for the lovers. Or, as Scott Peck, the author of the classic *The Road Less Traveled*", puts it, "at this point they begin either to dissolve the ties of their relationship or to initiate the work of real loving"[18].

Falling out of love is part of this cycle of falling in love, and the greater the immaturity the greater the probability. It does not mean an absence of love; rather, it means that the idealization of the *other* has lost much of its power and the lovers are coming down from the mountain of romance to the ground of reality. They have begun to see each other as they are in reality. And this "may prove to be somewhat melancholic"[19].

This melancholy is a wound and romantic love is able to inflict it on us precisely because of our feelings of inadequacy: we do not believe enough in ourselves; we do not really trust we are important; we don't believe we are loved enough, that others will like or accept us as we are. Sometimes we feel we are not good enough. No matter how wonderful our parents and families are, we grow up with these feelings that we are not complete, we are fundamentally alone, and we go in search of something or someone to complete us, in direct and indirect ways. These deficiencies are what psychologists call needs. Christianity attributes this lack to the effect of original sin, that event by which we lost our wholeness in and union with God. These needs express the more generalized restlessness of the human heart[20].

Now, what often happens in the experience of falling in love is that this *other*, the beloved or the lover, evokes the image of someone who will fulfil these needs, and lift us out of our existential loneliness. He or she responds to my needs and makes me feel like a somebody, accepted, adorable, loveable, and special. Then the lover can say, "with her, I really feel like a man, wonderful and strong"; and the beloved says, "he makes me feel special; he is *everything* to me"! Aldo

Carotenuto expresses this unconscious dynamic well: "If I feel divided and I also feel the impulse to achieve wholeness, and if there is only one person who personifies my potential, then that person actually becomes my hope, the incarnation of a possibility that only he or she can make actual. Thus we say, 'I can't live without you'"[21]. And that is their true feeling; they can't live without each other because each holds the promise for the fulfilment of the deep needs of the other. That is why love releases so much emotion, energy and life in us, those energies that have been bottled up by years of search for the one who will love us and reflect ourselves back to us or the one on whom we will pour our love in the hope of receiving back love. Now, we can go on living for life has, at last, become meaningful and interesting.

These same feelings which are true of the lovers are also the source of this wound, this baptism by fire. You will notice that in this event of falling in love, it is not totally the other who has seduced me; it is more my desires and needs which I expect to be fulfilled by him or her. The lover or the beloved merely offers the bait; he or she is the instrument and the incentive "but it is something personal, something within me, that bites the hook"[22]. Sooner or later the lover or the beloved starts to prove unable to fulfil those needs, and this is often disappointing.

In being unable to fulfil our expectations the lovers assert their individuality; they assert that they are different from us. He does not always like what I like, and she has particular tastes that annoy him. These differences were not seen when the lovers were drunk with romantic passion. The realization that the beloved is an individual with particular idiosyncrasies may feel like a sword that pierces through the idealized image of her in the consciousness of the lover. Reality dawns! That realization feels like a disappointment, a disappointment that feels like a deceit; a bad decision. Then we become resentful and hostile, irritable and irritated, and we even begin to think that we don't need the other[23]. But the *other* is not really the problem; I am the problem: I have been seduced by my own expectations so that I idealized and overestimated my lover or beloved, and I am disappointed. This baptism is a stepping stone to the transformation of romantic love and lovers, which is what we want to discuss in the remaining chapter.

Love has to deal with this aspect of our predicament. We all have different needs, and someone will appear before us carrying the promise of fulfilling them. Then we fall in love, and with time, we will also be baptised by fire and fall out of it. If we are lucky, we respond to the call for transformation, otherwise we live with the wounds that can sometimes turn into serious hate that can make our lives miserable. There is a mutual satisfaction in romantic love. It is the realisation that the lover has saved his beloved from a life of desperation, the desperate search for a lasting fulfilment of love's desire. The beloved also experiences this saving of her lover. A mutual gratefulness is the result if love is authentic, and the authenticity is proved by the ability of love to withstand these real and potential changes.

Betrayal and Abandonment

Not only do we get disappointed in our love life at certain moments, but there is also another wound of love, which remains always a possibility in all romantic love relationships – the fact that there can be betrayal and abandonment. So many love dramas, songs, novels, and books have been written on this theme. Yet, when we fall in love, no one ever thinks of this possibility, otherwise we may not be able to love.

When disappointment sets in; when the fragility and particularity of the beloved become more obvious, the lovers face a new set of experiences that confront them. These experiences are the occasions they need to readjust their idealized images of themselves and become more attuned to the hard facts of life and of the weaknesses of our human nature. On a more existential level, these experiences are a concrete reminder to the lovers of the transitoriness of most things in life, and the challenge to get to the essential. The intense and sweet feelings of love always have a sense of eternity in them, but the realization that the beloved or the lover is different makes us aware of the illusion of this feeling of eternity.

Some can't take this disappointment, this new awareness that shakes the sweet feelings that love provides. Whenever we refuse or reject this reality the dark side of ourselves and of love itself may be given the opportunity to take over our lives and the love relationship so that the lover or the beloved, without knowing, opens the door for a new lover or beloved to come in because he or she promises new life and hope, and helps the lovers to deny the reality facing them. The new person is always timely: he or she comes at the time the lovers are most vulnerable, when the original ardour of love is waning. Before this time, every other person existed but not like the lover or the beloved. Thoughts and feelings are focused on him or her. But when the intense feelings begin to confront reality, the eyes of the lovers are opened, and other persons now could assume a greater presence in their consciousness, and any one is a potential new "lover".

The arrival of a new person could lead to one of two consequences. First, it can be the means for the lovers to realize the beauty and validity of those good moments they had shared together. The new person is experienced as one *not like* the lover or the beloved. This experience sends the person back to the loved one. In that sense, betrayal is a kind of sounding board for the lovers to appreciate the love that had animated their lives. When this happens, the new lover unintentionally serves as a kind of catalyst that sets the motion for growth of the lovers and their relationship. Betrayal shatters the relationship, and out of the ruins, the lovers rebuild themselves more solidly and realistically. It is in this sense that betrayal, just like any of our transgressions, can serve as a *felix culpa*, a happy fall that leads to transformation[24].

The second consequence of betrayal is the break-up of the relationship: the lover or the beloved has gone after this new person in a way that indicates that the previous relationship feels like an obstacle to experiencing the new life that the new person promises. The relationship breaks up and breaks also the souls of both the lover and the beloved, but especially that of the one betrayed. The life experienced together, the joys and meanings shared together, have suddenly been shut down. The abandoned feels lost, pierced to the very depth of her soul and left to mourn her life all alone; no kind of consolation is adequate because each love relationship is unique[25].

The dividing sword of betrayal and abandonment is always present in a love relationship as a high possibility right from the day we fall in love, but the sweet feelings of love tend to drown it out. However, when the first disappointment surfaces, the possibility becomes more present; the lovers become more aware of it. This is an aspect of our predicament: since we carry our weaknesses, our shadows, and our lacks, we may be overtaken by them anytime so that that which used to be an experience of life and joy may end up in betrayal and abandonment. We may not avoid this possibility because "when we fall in love we start something that will soon get beyond our control and take its own course. Love contains the premises and the promises of eternity, but also the germ of annihilation"[26]. The abandoned lover precisely lives this annihilation. She feels completely let down; the meaning and security of her life are taken away, and she is left alone on an island which she alone inhabits. She may be surrounded by other people but her inner world is totally lacerated and in utter desolation. Life has become meaningless because all that has been constructed has crumbled. At the very extreme of this experience, such persons can get into clinical depression, commit suicide, kill the lover who betrayed them and the new person, or at best, become heavy drinkers or take to any of those lifestyles that depict total distrust towards life and persons.

There are two forms of abandonment: explicit and implicit. The explicit kind of abandonment happens when the lovers break up in fact so that the new person is shown for who he or she is. This form of abandonment is known publicly and the abandoned lover or beloved is not in doubt as to whether he or she has been abandoned. In explicit abandonment, the lovers have clearly left each other. The honesty and openness of explicit abandonment is a help to the abandoned because the true situation is clear to him or her to deal with in any way that is available.

Implicit abandonment is the more confusing, terrible, and emotionally sapping. It is the situation in which one of the lovers has withdrawn former emotional ties and invested it in a secret lover, the new "lover" that has no face. The abandoned lover struggles to make sense of a confused situation: communication is now rare and often very superficial; there is difficulty in being together and talking as used to happen before; their faces no longer glow when they are together; and their meeting is marked by a kind of generalized irritability and complaints.

Those lovers who have courage can deal with their changed internal state in a healthy manner, that is, letting their loved one know about their internal condition, how they are experiencing unease and diminished enthusiasm in their love relationship. Then both of them can work through the situation, identifying the difficulties, which oftentimes revolve around shattered expectations. The arrival of a new person, both the one with a face and the one without a face, signals a kind of deadlock in a relationship which has been either neglected or denied. Or it could be that the concerned lover does not have the courage to face the situation.

The possibility of betrayal and abandonment shows that love is full of risks. But these are risks worth taking because it is the experience of love that challenges us most to become adults, mature and aware of both ourselves and the life we live as human beings. Above all, love is a worthy risk to be taken because it is the venerable avenue through which our weaknesses, fears, and insecurity come out clearly to the consciousness so that we can know them and integrate them in our personality, if we choose.

Falling in Love with Someone Who does not love Me as I love Him/Her

The possibility that we may fall in love with someone who does not love us as much is another aspect of our predicament as human beings, and it follows from the preceding one. It poses a great deal of trouble that romantic love has to face. It would be a most astonishing thing in the world if everybody were to find his or her soulmate, that special man or woman with whom we are destined to drink the love potion of Eros together and face the challenges of living and growing. But desire is often very unrealistic. This would be possible if we did not have our psychological liabilities that feed on our human predicament.

The reason why we could fall in love with someone who does not really love us as much as we love them is because our psychological needs are as different and varied as our faces are. Though human needs are the same everywhere and in every person, their intensity differs from person to person. In some it is the intense desire for beauty, in others it is for intelligence, and in others still, it is for money or social status. These lacks seek for satisfaction in persons who appear to carry them, and this happens unconsciously, and all the time.

Take a simple example. Amanda is a young woman who is beautiful but not quite intelligent. This lack makes her feel inferior before some young women in school. A very handsome young man, Adam, falls in love with her, but she does not respond because she knows how poorly he performs in school; a weak mind like him will not fill her lack. Adam's presence is a nuisance to Amanda. Then one day during an academic conference, she sees Titus, a very smart young man in the engineering department. He is not quite handsome, but everybody knows he is a star in school. Amanda loses her head for him. She goes after him, seeks to talk with him, goes to dance with him. Titus merely likes Amanda but is not crazy about her as she is about him. Though Amanda makes him feel good especially because she is beautiful, he does not experience deep emotions towards her. You can see that Amanda can lead Titus into the depth of her very soul by telling him everything about her, and he may be very reluctant to allow her inside his inner world. While Titus ravishes Amanda she has not been able to shake or penetrate his emotional world. As long as Amanda goes after Titus who is less interested in her, she remains a captive to him. But there are persons who prefer to be captives to people like Titus in their lives as long as his presence gives them some edge over others. Now, it is possible that the persistence of Amanda may eventually shake Titus and he falls for her. It is always a possibility without guarantee.

This helps us understand why some people could fall in love many times, and each time with a person who promises to fulfil a lack. Most importantly, it sheds light on how our desires draw us to certain persons with different gifts ranging from the colour of hair, hairstyle, structure of body, of legs, of teeth, of eyes, to those with money, intelligence, fame, those who are sensitive, strong, caring, patient, and even those who are aggressive and menacing. The range is as wide and different as our lacks.

But the experience of the *other* as that person who lifts me up and makes me feel special may not be requited in equal intensity, as in the case of Amanda and Titus. Because Amanda *needs* Titus to feel important, special, and like a somebody, she is ready to endure any kind of mistreatment from him. In this form of relationship, dialogue is difficult because the person who is needed does not necessarily need the one who needs him. The one who seems to be in greater need engages herself in monologue with her desires or with the fantasized image of the desired lover who is unavailable.

This kind of relationship exists among some people and causes many frustrations. At a certain point in the relationship, Amanda will begin to complain that Titus is hardhearted for failing to recognize all the sacrifices she makes in their relationship, and Titus may snub her or, at best, be nice to her. But she does not want courtesy; she wants love! Yet, she may be too stubborn to realize that their communication is very superficial and that Titus is emotionally distant from her. Her intense need to feel important around the intelligent Titus does not allow her to see it. This kind of love relationship is a potential place for different forms of control and abuse. Honest communication can set such persons free. But in most cases, people like Amanda are undaunted in their neediness and are ready to suffer abuse provided the Tituses and their likes allow them in their company.

Attitudes of Men and Women towards Love and Sex

Our human predicament in love relationship is also expressed in the fact that the attitudes of men and women toward love and sex often are different. Experience tells us that men and women could have different understanding and approach to the issues of love and sex. For instance, Giddens observes that right from the very beginning, boys see sexual exploits and conquests as a demonstration of male capability such that "first sexual experience is a plus, a gain"[27]. The implication is that loss of virginity for boys is considered "a misnomer"[28]. For girls, on the other hand, loss of virginity, then as now, is experienced as something that is given up. And the question is always "with whom?" This question is important for girls because the experience of sex is often a kind of indication of or prelude to a future romantic life[29].

This exposes a substantial divide in the attitude of men and women towards love and sex which is expressed in the affirmations that men always want sex and women want love. In a survey he carried out with his students in the university, Russell Vannoy found out that nearly 80% of the young women "clearly preferred sex with someone who loved them". And for the young men, the opposite was the case: slightly less than 20% "found deep emotional involvement to be of any significant importance"[30]. In other words, most men want sex, quick and direct; for most women, even if they are to have it, it must be with someone whom they love and who loves them.

This perhaps explains the promiscuous tendency found more among men than among women. It also explains why women are hurt more in love relationships. When most men tend to want sex, quick and direct and circumvent the demands of love, and most women seek love, it is obvious there will be conflicts because their desires are different, even though they appear to speak the same language of love. In the concrete, it indicates that most women will tend to doubt apparent gestures of love from men because they fear it is just sex they want and not a true, demanding, and lasting relationship.

But most importantly, this attitude shows the existential predicament of men, the long journey they need to make in order to enter into the vulnerable world of love and be in touch with the desires of their hearts that goes beyond and deeper than the "quick fix" of sex. Because of this particular tendency to have quick sex, most men have tended to avoid the demands of true love and have denied their need for love from women. And sometimes if a man allows himself to get down to the vulnerable ground of self-revelation in a love relationship with a woman, other men taunt him as being foppish and under the spell of woman power[31]. As a consequence, most men have become alien to the experience of love and the genuine demands of growth it makes and become rather experts in the "techniques of seduction and conquest"[32]. That is why Stephen Levine notes that an important developmental challenge for men is to override their sexual preoccupations to learn about women as persons[33].

On the other hand, some women also tend to exploit this attitude of men so that they can use sex to manipulate and deceive some men into thinking that genuine relationship is happening between them. Some women also are too keen to seek love through a kind of sexual appeasement of men. Hence, the difference in these attitudes of men and women towards sex and love poses a real difficulty, and the more immature we are, the more these differences widen and become more polarized.

Both men and women need to love and to be loved. But it is generally the case that women are more accepting of their need than men who, oftentimes, are reluctant to acknowledge their emotional dependence on women, and mask it with their achievements and the piles of their "amorous conquests"[34]. This harms them more than it does women because they shield themselves from the experience of their vulnerability and inner nakedness which love calls for. This shield is what the experience of love breaks and leads them into the secured place of genuine psychological intimacy. Love calls forth the man inside to see himself, his limits and goodness, his sins and virtues. The power of love represented in the beloved can bring greater growth and inner freedom if one honestly engages oneself in it.

Love entails Work in Self-Knowledge

We have been examining the various aspects of our human predicament which enter into our relationship of love. This examination is meant to demonstrate that the complexity, ambiguity, and confusion we experience in love and sex have their origin in our human nature and the way this human nature expresses itself in our various personalities. The implication is that love always starts off as this intense desire, but, like everything that generates life and lasting joy in human life, it demands work and perseverance.

The work that love needs should be understood more in terms of the work the lovers need to do on themselves as love takes them deeper and deeper into their souls and confronts them with the reality of human life. This important work is knowledge of the self and growth to greater maturity. Persons should try to know themselves well, why they have certain feelings in a relationship, why some attitudes and features of those they love provoke specific feelings in them. Love itself challenges the lovers in this exercise; and it is at the background of every step of transformation that the love experience takes them.

Chapter Six

From Romance to Committed Love

It was Aldo Carotenuto who noted that in romantic love, we human beings have developed a love dimension that is against nature, and we do not have a genetic makeup that can take care of it[1]. This is because the experience of love is so strong that it creates a kind of upheaval in which the lovers come face to face with a power that is beyond logic, beyond the familiar way of thinking and living. It is both a risk and an adventure. Though a wonderful life-changing and life-giving experience, love is always accompanied by fear and trepidation because "we have not mastered it"[2]. And because we have not mastered it, "the worst pains and sufferings that we inflict and are inflicted upon us mostly occur in the realm of love"[3], for love can so easily hurt both the lover and the beloved, and this, we cannot explain.

We should not be surprised that we don't have the gene wired in our system that will be able to handle the high energy of romantic love because we human beings are not just body, as Carotenuto writes[4]. Unless we recognize the spiritual dimensions of our life as human beings, it will be difficult to understand and manage the message of Eros. The transformation of love and the lovers must happen at the moral and religious dimensions of our lives, that dimension where we experience ourselves as persons of freedom and choice.

Love and Sex: Levels at which We live

Since we are not simply objects but embodied spirits, human subjects, we live our lives at different levels, distinct but unified in our being as persons: we live our lives at the psycho-physical, the psycho-social, and the psycho-spiritual levels. The word psyche that is hyphenated to the physical, social, and spiritual, is meant to show that it is the same self, this same person, who is acting at these levels. At the psychophysical level, we attend to our biological needs, but as I said in the last chapter, with purpose and intention. At the psychosocial level, we attend to the demands of our social life, and at the psychospiritual level, we are faced with giving ultimate meaning to our entire life. And without this meaning, our life can be hopeless and less interesting. In other words, it is this psychospiritual dimension of our lives that is at the foreground as we go about our lives; it exercises a leading role in our lives such that what happens at that level is amplified in other levels[5]. This is not difficult to understand: just imagine yourself having all the food you need and having all the pleasures you wish to enjoy (the psychophysical), and having thousands of people with whom you connect (psychosocial), but still feel that your life is meaningless (the psychospiritual). You notice immediately that all these things, though important and necessary, are subject to our experience of fulfilment in life.

This is why our behaviour, our life as human beings, is more than satisfying our biological desires or merely a striving to be important in the world and among others. This means then that the search for meaning or fulfilment, which is the deepest yearning of every human being, cannot be found at the level of basic needs and instincts, but at that level which we have called the spiritual; that level where we make decisions and choices that agree with our notion of a meaningful life. This further means that love, that affective state that seeks the good of the other, though heavily evident in our bodies and our relationship, seeks to be connected to the spiritual dimension, that dimension where we are concerned with the ultimate meaning of our lives. In actual fact, the yearning to love and to be loved is a deep yearning for meaning, for completeness, for fulfilment, for self-acceptance. This yearning is what many men and women, educated and uneducated, sophisticated and simple, have, throughout ages and places, identified as our desire for God, the Source of Love[6]; it "is the essence of the human spirit; it is the origin of our highest hopes and most noble dreams"[7].

Our desire to love and to be loved is fundamentally a spiritual yearning in disguise, a yearning for union with God, that absolute *Other* who made us for Himself so that our hearts are restless until they rest in him, as St. Augustine says. Carotenuto expresses it well, even if he did not recognize it, when he said that love "is intrinsically the experience of absence, an absence is connected to nostalgia. It is as if throughout our lives we continually felt a deep dissatisfaction. We are moved by a sense of the infinite, whereas our achievements are always limited".[8] In romantic love we have an experience of the infinite and of abundance of life because we yearn for that infinite life with nostalgia. But then, we tend to misrepresent this deeper longing with sexual satisfaction. We satisfy this desire for infinite with the finite, and we get messed up: we demand from Eros more than it can provide. The most Eros could do is to provide us with a glimpse of that infinite.

Here we can understand the confusion and conflicts experienced in love, sex, and relationship. It often happens that we unknowingly search for completeness, meaning and fulfilment in the intense desires of Eros and of sexual passion. The ecstasy that accompanies romantic love promises a life without end, an everlasting and blissful experience of wholeness and serenity in the arms of the beloved or the lover. But sooner or later, the ambivalences of our human nature emerge and bring us back to reality. Then our expectations and dreams of the beloved hit rock and our passion is lifted. When passion diminishes, dreams of the beloved or the lover dissolve like the morning dew and the lovers come back to the stark reality and bemoan their disillusionment. The search may continue for some, perhaps till the twilight of their lives. Or the lovers take a step forward, going from the consuming love of Eros to true love that is founded in commitment.

Because of these problems associated with romantic love Scott Peck believes that romantic love is an illusion. He claims that romantic love is unreal because it is usually a sex-linked experience, and also because the experience is temporary[9]. The only credit he gives to it is that "falling in love is a trick that our genes pull on our otherwise perceptive mind to hoodwink or trap us into marriage"[10]. This position does not seem to me to be a fair representation of the whole experience of romantic love. Everyone agrees that the bloom of romantic love may wane after some time depending on the level of maturity and on the point the persons are in their relationship. But this does not make romantic love unreal or an illusion just as much as our efforts to make the world a better place is not an illusion despite the fact that we shall die one day and leave everything behind. Romantic love is an experience that goes deeper than the merely sexual. It is more a pointer to the bigger picture of who we are: created for union with God, with other human beings, and with the whole of God's creation. It is an experience of our own mystery as human beings. The illusion in romantic love happens when we try to make romance an end in itself just as we suffer illusion and disappointment when we pursue the goods of this world as mere ends in themselves. Eros stirs up the sexuality in us, which is the energy we have to relate with others, with God, and with the whole creation. Romantic lovers get into trouble when the fires of our sexuality, our capacity to relate, become confused with or reduced to the genitals.

Growth in the capacity to love, therefore, demands that people should grow and integrate the romantic aspect of their relationship[11]. That overwhelming aspect of romantic relationship is not sustainable for a very long time because we don't have an infinite source of energy to feed it and meet the demands. Moreover, life is larger than these intense feelings. There are other values and duties that we need to attend in our lives. Lovers need to develop deep trust in themselves that can let them be free, and yet, with deep affection for each other. Oftentimes, holding onto the consuming feelings of romance only can be a sign of distrust between the lovers. It can also express some emptiness and insecurity. As long as romantic lovers remain and hope to remain in that pool of intense feelings they will find it difficult to settle into a fulfilling and lasting relationship, which love desires. All that will happen is drama, love adventures, intense love scenes, jealousies, and even betrayals when passion lifts from the beloved. To settle down in a lasting relationship requires a keen awareness of the fact that our deepest desire for love and for union is spiritual; it is a desire to share oneself with another at the very depth; it is a desire for God. Romantic lovers must therefore grow into existential soulmates and become friends if they want their love to last.

Love desires Existential Affinity in Friendship

There is in each of us a place in our souls where we are truly ourselves; where we are in touch with what shapes our lives; where we nurture the visions that drive us through life; where we have laboured and articulated the strands that constitute the dimensions that give meaning to our lives. At this very place, we live our convictions, of what is right and what is wrong, what should be and what should not be. From this place also, we have a glimpse of the fact that human life is not simply eating and drinking, making money and having sex, acquiring power and titles; human life is an adventure, a kind of quest for the sense of life. At this deep level we listen to the agitations of our hearts, the dissatisfactions we feel, our illusions and disappointments, and we raise serious questions about them.

When we get to this place, then we realize how lonely we can be, and how love relationships can be truly superficial unless they take us to this level. Not anyone can penetrate that place because "where what is most precious lies is also where we are the most vulnerable to violation"[12]. This is the level which the love that starts off as romantic experience seeks to lead the lovers, to that guarded place in their souls where they share the same vision of life, common values that give direction to their lives, deep convictions of life that give meaning to their lives. It is this existential affinity between their souls that romantic love seeks to establish between them. When love leads lovers to this level, then they really can "sleep" with each other whether there is sexual union or not[13]. The other, the beloved, in this existential affinity, has become a kindred spirit, a real friend, a true companion with whom life's questions are raised and answers sought. And this is the place where we become intensely aware of the spiritual dimension of our life; of our restlessness outside God. This existential affinity is the greatest and deepest union lovers can experience. It is the level of friendship where there is warmth, affection, connection at both the level of values and emotions. Here the individuals are completely themselves.

Eros, though good and great an experience, must be transcended. But before it can lead lovers to this inner aspect of their being, they must wean themselves of the dramas of the romantic; the lovers must draw themselves beyond their physical appeal which feeds the sexual passion. This is what the fading of passion, the disappointments, the falling out of love, and the illusions, accomplish in romantic love, and they signal that the dramatic phase is over. These events, if understood and worked through, lead the lovers to the discovery of themselves as trusted companions, as kindred spirits, as true friends, as spiritual pilgrims. And if they are married, they rediscover their physical beauty in a new way that does not shout with the intense demands of Eros. If they are not married, they discover a more solid bonding in their common values, a kind of bonding that does not suffer the affliction of romantic possessiveness. Love at this level has become less troublesome and more peaceful for the lovers. When romantic love fails to go beyond the romantic, especially when the passion begins to fade, it can open the door to betrayal. If betrayal is not an inclined alternative, the lovers may become two lonely islands living together. But if they decide to give up the romantic affairs and refuse to be entrapped in a "tired love" or seek the self-defeating alternative of betrayal, they open themselves up to the great experiences of personal transformation. This opening up is aided by two things: first, that love is lived as a commitment, and secondly, that commitment is lived also in the background of a spiritual life.

Commitment: from Falling in Love to Choosing to love

When persons fall in love they seem to have no control over it. Whether it is the sudden experience of falling in love or the one in which the lovers had had some time to build up their relationship, romantic love is something we usually fall into. No one knows the time or the place or with whom it is going to happen. As Peck rightly notes, "we are as likely to fall in love with someone with whom we are obviously ill matched as with someone more suitable"[14]. It is so easy to love the beloved or the lover because the sweet feelings of Eros make everything beautiful and perfect. But as the romantic passion starts to wane and the lovers begin to realize their differences, things may no longer be as sweet and easy as they used to be. The lovers then must *choose to continue to love* each other. Where choice used to be effortless, one must make a concerted effort to choose to continue to love This decision to continue to love each other *in spite* of the diminished romantic passion or its absence, *in spite* of the differences between them, is the foundation of a committed relationship. From this moment, love has become a duty, a choice, more than it is a feeling; love has passed through those aesthetic and emotional regions of our personality where the romantic resides to that aspect of our personality where values are recognized and decisions are carried out based on them. It is in this region of the personality that "true commitments are born and grow"[15]. With the decision to go on loving despite lack of those consuming feelings, the lovers have consciously embarked on the long journey of both human and spiritual maturity. The mystery experienced in the romantic phase of the relationship shall now be explored and experienced in a new way that draws them deeper into their very nature as both body and spirit, and as children of God made for communion. Each seeks the good of the other whether they still feel the intense feelings of Eros or not.

It is from this perspective that we can note that every authentic relationship that nurtures the human being, body and soul, is somehow agapeic. In agape, we love the other for his or her sake irrespective of how we feel about him or her. We make effort to seek the good of another whether we "feel" like doing so or not. When we love in this way, we somehow transcend ourselves, our preferences and feelings. In transcending ourselves, we are also deeply fulfilled as human beings, as children of God, and as true members of the human family. This choice to continue to love at all costs is guided and sustained mostly by our moral and religious values.

Guided by Moral and Religious Values

What comes out clearly from this reflection so far is that the movement from a dramatic romantic love to a lasting and more stable relationship of love implies some kind of death: a dying to the values and the loyalties of the romantic love with its heat of sexual passion and its impossible demands; a renunciation of the desire to unite permanently with the beloved in such a way that could alienate the lovers from living with others in society; a realization that the sweet feelings of attraction will not always be around. Consciousness must undergo some changes, some transformation. It involves the sacrifice of the sweet taste of the romantic, and this is painful. However, the lovers can agree to bear the pain for the purpose of personal growth and transformation. And there is one thing that this progressive transformation needs: commitment. Commitment helps withstand the tendency to slip back into the search for meaning at the wrong level; it is commitment to the enduring values of the other in a stable friendship that enables the persons to withstand the pull to return to inauthentic ways of living and relating; it is commitment to the discipline of chastity that helps the lovers withstand the flirtations of the generalized tendencies of the body; it is commitment that enables romantic lovers to deal with the predicaments which our human nature presents. Again, the ability to commit oneself in a relationship is dependent on our level of maturity. What this implies is that individuals should make serious effort to grow in their personalities, in self-knowledge.

Romantic relationship asks for commitment from the lovers, and not just affection. The tendency today is to assume that the single and essential element in a true relationship is romance and sexual passion, so that John tells Sandra that a relationship with her which excludes sex is useless and empty. This assumption is one of the reasons why we can be so disappointed with relationships, disgusted and full of distrust for the other, and even sceptical about any relationship. Those flowering words of love are often not believed because it could be the passion that has lifted from another person that may be hiding behind them.

Commitment to sexual pleasure does not and cannot replace commitment to a person. You wonder why some people are forever seeking lovers even to their grave, and go on picking and dumping people along the path of life, marrying and divorcing as and when they feel like, especially in the industrialized parts of the world. They wound the people they are involved with but are also wounded themselves in their inability to connect at a deeper level with their so-called lovers. Hence, they can feel very empty and lonely because they have not given their hearts truly to any concrete person or to God.

Morality of sexual passion contrasts with the morality of commitment to real persons in their beauty and ugliness, gifts and limitations. Our heart seeks to be given to love, but to someone that is real. That is why people who are unable to commit themselves to real persons can feel in their life a kind of motion without specific direction even if they have lovers all over the place and enough money to maintain them. It is commitment that the heart of each person yearns for: someone who is devoted and committed to me and on whom I can depend; someone whom I can trust and share my stories with; someone who can accompany me faithfully on my journey of life; someone who does not think I am an angel; someone who accepts my liabilities and those of nature; someone who does not demand that I look young all the days of my life; someone who understands that the economy has changed; someone who knows that we are connected to the vast world of human beings guided by certain values; someone who shares with me those cherished values and deep convictions about life; someone who is ready to get deeper with me into that sacred place in which we feel at home as kindred spirits, as friends, as children of God.

When romantic lovers truly commit themselves to each other, they can deepen their relationship beyond the appeals of sex and body, and so are empowered to deal with the tendency to seek substitute love. Commitment is also nurtured by authentic communication in which the lovers are able to express themselves without too much judgment. It is this communication that enables them to see through their unconscious desires and lacks, so that they can understand the kind of expectations they have of themselves, however realistic and unrealistic they are.

In order to be able to commit themselves to each other, romantic lovers need the guidepost provided by moral and religious values. Romantic lovers are often helpless in their situation; the stirs of emotion can sweep everything along with it, including the lovers themselves. The moral and religious values of chastity, of sexual expression in marriage, of fidelity, and of respect for the dignity of persons as children of God, help the romantic lovers to hold in check the wild tide of romantic feelings and emotions, giving them direction and purpose.

Commitment entails Waiting

There is always a feeling of urgency and immediacy that surrounds romantic love, which makes the lovers feel they have lost their bearing, and the demand of union and sexual expression could be felt as a kind of fate in some persons. The tension this creates can feel unbearable. Yet, it is bearable; it is bearable for a purpose, the purpose of commitment, of a lasting relationship. But most importantly, it is bearable because, as Milan

Kundera rightly notes, we live in a world in which most things occur once, and given the ambiguities in sex and in our human nature, we try and bear the tension of the moment for a more durable relationship, for a life that stretches to the point of our death. What we want now must always look up to what we generally want in life, and what we want in life must be reasonable. Inability to look at life in this manner has ruined many people and many love relationships: it has led to impulsive decisions and choices, and a kind of immediate experience that emptied the soul rather than filling it. It is in this sense that chastity is not simply a sexual concept; it expresses an attitude of waiting, of living the tension of now, for a purpose; it "means to experience all things respectfully and to drink them in and when we are ready for them. We break chastity when we experience anything irreverently or prematurely"[16].

Romantic lovers need to cultivate the discipline of waiting if they hope to enjoy their love and grow in it. But their waiting must have a reason. They don't wait because someone has asked them to do so or because they are afraid of something. They wait because their lives as human beings, who are moral and religious, demand it. Their ability to wait for a reason is part of the challenges they must face in order to reach a reasonable level of maturity and personal integration. And it is the moral and religious values that help them wait. The liberalization of sex that is everywhere today is anything but liberating; it fights directly against people's ability to endure the tension of sexual desire for a durable experience of love and relationship. In the third stage of his intellectual development Sigmund Freud, often associated with the free expression of the repressed sexual energy, said that when sexual satisfaction triumphs, when people are unable to wait, love is easily eliminated and "the death instinct has a free hand for accomplishing its purposes"[17]. When love is not lived as commitment, and the lovers are unable to exercise the discipline of waiting until the right time, then the death instinct, feeding on those aspects of human predicament we outlined in the last chapter, draws them onto their own destruction. The right time is decided not only by our individual readiness and maturity; it is judged also by the moral and religious values that are the foundation on which our lives as human beings and our societies depend: the value of human dignity, respect for persons as children of God, love and fidelity, honesty and trust in relationship, the stability of marital life, care of children, care of future generations, value of the human race, and so on. When these values are not respected, persons and societies are under serious threat. And you can see how impatience in romantic love can easily set the motion whose end may not be foreseen in that split moment of sexual ecstasy. Carlo Carretto, the great Italian spiritual writer, and one of the greatest spiritual writers of our time once said: "God is telling us: learn to wait – wait – wait for your God, wait for love, be patient with everything. Everything that is worthwhile must be waited for!"[18]

Coming Home to God: Eros and the Spiritual Life

The decision to give up looking for meaning and fulfilment in the heat of romantic love and, instead, to search for it at the right level of existence, expresses the need to cultivate a spiritual life, a life that "is concerned with ultimate meanings and values, but it is incarnated in human encounters and circumstances"[19]. Christian spiritual life is a life of love. Jesus revealed to us that we are all meant for love, and this love is God himself. When this love of God fills our hearts, it forms the ground of the meaning of our lives, our decisions and actions.

This love is what theologians call grace. In pouring His love in our hearts, God invites us to relate with Him because He is a person, and only persons can relate with one another. Christianity is therefore not a morality: it is the following of a person, Jesus Christ, in a transforming relationship of love. He takes His place at the center of our lives such that "whether I am married or single, my friendship and love for God becomes the most real of all my relationships. He becomes the center of my life and, because he is other than me, outside of my personality, I now have a new orientation away from myself. I begin to live for God, not for self: away from myself and towardS the Master of my life, God"[20]. The relationship affects all the person is and does: his or her choices, decisions, relationship with persons, thoughts, and even imagination. Nothing is left out under the influence of this relationship. On the whole, life is meaningful and the fruits of the Holy Spirit are verifiable in the person: love, joy, peace, humour, serenity even in suffering and pain, patience, kindness, goodness, gentleness, and so on. This state is not a static one; it is a dynamic state that is nurtured constantly in prayer and through prayer and the sacraments. Committed love is when the romantic lovers, having wandered far away to islands and wild forests in search of wholeness, completeness and meaning, gradually come home to God in the experience of the love that does not dramatize, the love that heals, fills up, and energizes one to value others and serve them for their sake.

It is the love of God that purifies and sustains the tide of Eros. It holds in check the wild desires and demands that could come from Eros and channels them towardS Love Itself. In this way, the often godly voice of Eros can be recognised for what it is and given its proper place. The Christian life lived intensely as spiritual life enables Eros to retain its nature and introduces the lovers into that Love which transforms persons, relationships, and the human society. But to do this, certain steps are necessary.

First, life lived mostly at the level of Venus, that is, explicit sex, is hardly ready to engage itself in the process of full human and spiritual maturity. The person of the individual is befogged by the intense desire of Venus, so that all that stands in front of the person is an object that hears and satisfies the cry of Venus. This is what happens in sex markets and in those friendships in which sex is the central focus; where the so-called friends swear that there can be no love without sex. This is the voice of Venus and not Eros. The voice of Eros is fascinated with the beloved so that even when it is suggested that they cannot live together, say in marriage, "Eros never hesitates to say, 'Better this than parting. Better to be miserable with her than happy without her. Let our hearts break provided they break together'. If the voice within us does not say this, it is not the voice of Eros"[21]. There should be no confusion between Eros and Venus; their voices and preoccupations are different. The challenge at this level is to grow into the appreciation of the individual person; to really let oneself fall in love and focus on the person of the Beloved. You will notice the tension between sex and love, between Venus and Eros.

At the second step, Eros is challenged by the Christian spiritual life to respect God who is Love Himself in order to lead the lovers under its spell to genuine happiness and transformation. The tension here is between following the voice of Eros or the voice of God in His Christ. The real question which is the most fundamental in the spiritual life is this: whom do you serve, God or your earthly beloved? For where your treasure is, there your heart is, Jesus says. Lewis summarizes it: "Eros, without diminishing desire, makes abstinence easier. He tends, no doubt, to a preoccupation with the Beloved which can indeed be an obstacle to the spiritual life; but not chiefly a sensual pre-occupation"[22]. This kind of preoccupation is more advanced than the preoccupation of Venus.

Living a spiritual life does not diminish our humanity as some people are wont to believe. Again, the spiritual life is not really in complete opposition to Eros. After all, the stirs of Eros are the stirs of our sexuality, our capacity to relate with God, with our fellow human beings, and with the entire creation. When we lead an authentic spiritual life we reap the fruits of romantic love to the full. The reason is that the spiritual life prevents us from getting stuck in the ambivalences of the romantic aspect of a relationship; we transcend it when we open ourselves to the deeper desires of our hearts where God speaks to us and leads us to Himself and to our fulfilment as human beings. When this happens, we can identify those aspects of us we have repressed or not accepted, and which Eros has awakened. Then we struggle not to allow them to disrupt our lives. This may not always be successful, but we don't have to give up because it is the right thing to do in order to facilitate our growth as human beings.

It is not always easy to refuse the desires of the beloved or the lover. Sometimes the lovers would wish there were no God to be loved, respected or obeyed so that they could give free reign to their desires. This is understandable when people are in love. But life is larger than the intense feelings of Eros that tend to put the questions about tomorrow and of human life in the clouds. Learning to listen and hear the voice of God helps the lovers retain some focus. Moreover, it helps them also pay attention to the deeper desire of their heart beyond the beckoning of Eros. That desire is for a lasting and authentic intimacy. They will never regret it now or in the future for having given God an important place in their lives.

.

Conclusion

Dialogue between Eros and Chastity

In this book I have tried to examine the question of whether love should include sex or not. We saw that love can exist with or without sex. There are many kinds of sex without love as there are many kinds of love without sex. But the love that is called Eros or romantic love poses particular difficulty. It is a unique human experience. It gives life but also death, depending on how mature we are. In the second part of this study we saw the nature of the changes and transformation romantic lovers and romantic love need to undergo.

We must try to respect Eros. It is a unique human experience and occupies an important place in the life of any man or woman. But it has been a deep source of difficulty for many people, especially those who want to live intensely the spiritual life. Eros is a problem especially when it seeks union in sexual intercourse. Because of this, people consider Eros dangerous and in opposition to the spiritual life. They say that Eros is earthly, human, carnal, and less holy, and the spiritual life is heavenly, spiritual, and holy. The two are supposedly in opposition and every effort should be made to keep them apart. From this dualistic tendency, a lot of ascetic practices emerged, ranging from extreme dry fasting to different forms of laceration of the body in order to keep it subjected to the Spirit.

This dualistic thinking has produced two groups of individuals with extreme positions regarding Eros and chastity. The first group of individuals consists of the very pious persons who denigrate anything that suggests a meddling with the earthly and the 'merely' human such as drinking, going to parties, and having a friend of the opposite sex. According to this mindset, these things 'soil' the spirit and keep it fettered to the earth. Sexual desires are condemned and sometimes a good sign of spiritual growth would be the elimination of those desires. At the other extreme are those individuals who follow the more permissive ideology which holds that people should be allowed to be themselves, and express the natural instincts that God has given them. In this group are those who equate male-female relationship to having sex partners. These people believe that relationship with the opposite sex is impossible without genital expression.

These two extreme positions are both wrong for two reasons. First, they do not present our human nature well. That is, each denies an essential aspect of our lives. We are not either body or spirit, but both of them. So, Eros which stirs up our sexuality, our capacity for relationship, and our sexual desires cannot be reduced to sex as if we are only body. At the same time, we cannot denigrate Eros because of these stirrings as though we are only spirit. Eros carries the fire we need to relate to both human beings and to God. It is the passion of relatedness, and therefore, it is not simply sex. Secondly, these extreme positions are wrong because they hardly lead to interior freedom which a genuine and committed love generally brings.

The dualism between the body and the soul goes back to certain Greek philosophies. These philosophies state that the world of sensible experience is false and illusory; it is a semblance of the true reality and an obstacle to the human mind in search of true knowledge. Therefore, the body, being part of this sensible world, obstructs more than it helps in the achievement of true knowledge. For Plato, the body is a prison of the soul, and it "disturbs that clear working of the reason, spirit, and appetites by exposing the soul to a cascade of sensations"[1]. This philosophy has influenced many people in the past and today to believe that sexual desires are disgusting.

On the other hand, the ideology of sexual permissiveness conceives sex as a natural thing, an instinct like any other such as hunger and thirst to which people are entitled in order for them to experience the fullness of themselves. This ideology has its root in secular humanistic psychology that conceptualizes self-fulfilment in terms of the fullest expression of oneself in everything including sex so that any kind of inhibition of one's feelings is considered unhelpful to the person's growth and maturity. Whatever one feels will make one happy and fulfilled, one goes after it. Thus, sex is at last freed from taboos and inhibitions and people give themselves over to it. At last, people become more concerned with getting the greater enjoyment in sex than in loving, hence more and more techniques[2] in getting the best out of sex[3].

The conflict between these two extreme groups is not only evident in ordinary discussions, but also in their individual lifestyles: the one can be stiff, lifeless, and too worried about sexual taints that she spends more time warding off the thoughts about sex than abandoning herself serenely in the hands of God. He or she is afraid of any relationship because of the conflicts it may generate. The other has lost a sense of direction and has given himself or herself over to the drug of sex. They appear carefree; everything is allowed in their life. For him or her, life is a continuous motion of making and breaking commitments and promises: nothing should be permanent, including friendship. Commitment is important and lasts as long as they are getting their fill of pleasures. When such persons say they want to get settled in marriage, they mean a different thing: to get married like others and be part of the social structure. But deep down, it is not a commitment that demands everything they are and have: they are free to hop around from one sex partner to another.

In the first extreme position, one can find persons whose spiritual life lacks passion, what I call *Passionless Christianity*; a Christianity in which the struggle to keep oneself pure has put off relationship with Christ as a person, so that the energy spent in this struggle is so much as to drive out the joy of living. Often, such persons look stiff, rigid, and somehow worried and unhappy. Humour and liveliness have gone out of their lives. Most of their talks usually revolve around sex. The whole of Christianity is reduced to just keeping the sixth commandment. It is a preoccupation with the self that can become an impediment to personal development and to a true and transforming encounter with God in His Christ which leads to a total surrender of oneself completely to God. The unrelaxed life of some persons in this group puts people off; sometimes some of them can be unforgiving, too demanding of others, and unable to bear with the weaknesses of other people. They have become less human in trying to construct their own idea of holiness[4]. Their excessive concern with purity has crushed their lives, robbed it of its humanity, "its spontaneity, and many of its deep pleasures"[5]. And for those of them who appear to be happy and contented, it is often due to their pharisaic self-adulation: they are not like the rest of men and women. Again, it is the self that is at the center of worship.

In the second group we find the persons whose spiritual life is full of passion but no Christ, and I describe it as *Christless Passion*! Such persons are too sentimental, emotive, easily blown away by the latest spiritual talk; their spiritual values change from one moment to another, depending on who is talking to them. Their spiritual life is full of passion without Christ because they detest any kind of pain or suffering. They can be full of passion now, and in the next moment when they are sexually excited, they cannot bear the pain of having *to wait* until the true moment comes. When they are done with it, they may cry, curse the person and the time, and make all the right promises. But the next moment of excitement comes and suffering and pain are again driven out. For such persons, opportunities of sex should not be missed, and the pain involved in personal growth and following Christ is negotiable. It is the caress of Jesus they seek more than Jesus Himself, the one who obeyed His Father unto death on the cross. Individuals in this group believe so much in Eros and the emotions it carries. They often insist that all the desires of Eros must be obeyed and the sexual desires it awakens should be satisfied. But it is often the case that these individuals are more concerned with the sexual gratification of Venus than with the beloved of Eros. Hence, they can regard a life of chastity as old-fashioned and unreal.

These two extreme positions reflect the two faces of the question regarding love and sex, Eros and sexual purity. The problems may be different but they express one thing; namely, that the desires of Eros and chastity are yet to be integrated in our lives. We can live chaste lives as vowed celibates, unmarried persons, or as married people. In whatever state of life we are, we are confronted with the need to reconcile the passions of Eros and chastity. The struggle for this integration often leads to one of these extreme positions.

The integration of romantic passion and chastity is a true reflection of who we are as humans: body and soul. When we live with both aspects of us, we are who God truly meant for us to be. If we reject any of them, we are dividing ourselves. Eros is that passion of our sexuality which connects us to the whole of life, to persons, and to God. Chastity protects us from being reduced to just objects of sexual gratification. It is a bold assertion that we are spirit and body. Yet, the life of chastity may become an avenue to run away from or denigrate the fires of our sexuality.

This means that passion must not be denigrated; Eros must not be put down, it must not be regarded as satanic or from the devil. Eros is a gift; it comes from God. But it must obey God. It must not be allowed to make demands it cannot have. Eros asks for direction from moral and religious values; from the deep desires of lasting and stable friendship. Eros needs chastity to avoid wasting its passion, its fire for a passing moment, and leaving a deep wound in the soul. But sexual purity also needs the passion of Eros, the fire that Eros usually kindles. Without such passion, purity can become tasteless and without feeling. And this is dangerous. Passionless spirituality can become wicked and alienating without knowing, and passion without spirituality can be destructive of persons and societies.

It would seem that this problem is absent among married people. This is far from the truth. One of the most frequent disagreements married couples have revolves around sex such as when and how often! As each day passes, they have to deal with their different attitudes, moods and motivations towards the passions of Eros expressed in sexual intercourse. If they reflect on their experiences together, they will see their need to live a more transformed love and sexual experience. This is what their fidelity to each other is meant to achieve. Still more, it does not take long time for them to realize their need for a deeper life of union beyond sex. If they don't recognize this moment and try to stick to the passions of Eros, then they expose themselves to certain negative forces that impede their personal and spiritual development. If one of them decides that their sexual life should be eliminated completely for the sake of chastity in marriage, there will be problems. All this indicates that married couples should try to understand the stages of their love development and the necessary adjustments they need to make in order to further their personal and collective growth.

Eros and chastity, therefore, need integration, and the life of Jesus Christ is our model. During his life on earth, Jesus was consumed with a passion for God and for human beings, a passion in which his preoccupation was His father and our salvation. He had female friends but he remained chaste. Married people live life of chastity also when they remain faithful to their spouses and seek both their human and spiritual growth. There are many people in the past and today, Christians and non-Christians, who have lived this life of integrating the passion of Eros with the discipline of chastity. No matter how difficult it may appear to be, it is the life each of us is called to live if we are to mature fully as human beings, as children of God.

Notes

Chapter One

[1] A.S. Reber, *The Penguin Dictionary of Psychology*, London 1985.

[2] *The Oxford English Reference Dictionary*, ed. J. Pearsall & B. Trumble, 2nd Edition, Oxford UK, 1996.

[3] *Collins English Dictionary and Thesaurus*, Major New Edition, United Kingdom, 1995.

[4] A.S. Reber.

[5] W. Barclay, *New Testament Words*, Louisville, Kentucky, 1964, 15.

[6] Ibid., 18.

[7] Ibid., 20.

[8] Ibid., 21.

[9] F. Ferder & J. Heagle, *Tender Fires*, New York 2002, 29.

[10] Ibid.

[11] V.A. Sadock, Normal Human Sexuality and Sexual and Gender Identity Disorders, in B.J. Sadock & V.A. Sadock (Eds.) *Comprehensive Textbook of Psychiatry*, 7th ed. Philadelphia 2000, 1577.

[12] Congregation for the Doctrine of the Faith, *On the Collaboration of Men and Women in the Church and in the World*, May 31, 2004, nn. 2-3.

[13] See W.S. Pollack, "Fatherhood as a Transformation of the Self: Steps Toward a New Psychology of Men", *Review of Psychiatry* 18/5 (1999) 89-113, esp. 110.

[14] J.K. Baslwick & J.O. Balswick, *Authentic Human Sexuality*, Downers Grove, Illinois 1999, 14-15, see figure 1.1.

[15] T.S. Stein, Homosexuality and Homosexual Behaviour, in B.J. Sadock & V.A. Sadock (Eds.), 1608. For a detailed

information regarding the relationship between sexual orientation to a person's general sex role orientation and a person's erotic fantasies, see M.D. Storms, Theories of Sexual Orientation, *Journal of Personality and Social Psychology*, 38/5 (1980) 783-792.
[16] A.S. Reber, *The Penguin Dictionary of Psychology*.
[17] L. Sperry, *Sex, Priestly Ministry, and the Church*, Collegeville, Minnesota 2004, 3.

Chapter Two
[1] R. May, *Love and Will*, New York 1969, 38.
[2] D. von Hilderbrand, Sex, in *New Catholic Encyclopedia*, Vol. XIII, New York 1967, 147.
[3] R. Scruton, *Death-Devoted Heart: Sex and the Sacred in Wagner's Tristan and Isolde*, Oxford 2004, 137.
[4] J. Evola, *Metafisica del Sesso*, English translation, *Eros and the Mysteries of Love*, by Inner Traditions International, Rochester, Vermont 1983, 1991, 13.
[5] M.A. Friederich, Motivations for Coitus, *Clinical Obstetrics and Gynecology*, 13/3 (1970), 693.
[6] Ibid.

[7] J. Byrne, A Life of Chastity for the Kingdom of God: Problems and Perspectives, *Religious Life Review*, 21/97 (1982)194-195.
[8] M.A. Friederich, 697.
[9] Ibid., 698.
[10] Ibid.
[11] Ibid., 699.
[12] J. Byrne, 194.

Chapter Three
[1] A. Carotenuto, *Eros e Pathos: Margini dell'amore e della sofferenza*, English trans. *Shades of Love and Suffering*, tr. C. Nopar, Toronto 1989, 17-18.

[2] These citations come from Shakespeare's plays retold in story form for modern readers. B. Birch, *Shakespeare's Stories. Tragedies*, New York, New Jersey 1988, 33.

[3] Ibid., 46.

[4] Carotenuto, 17.

[5] J. Bédier, *The Romance of Tristan and Isolde*, tr. H. Belloc & P. Rosenfeld, New York 1945.

[6] Ibid., 41-42.

[7] Ibid., 62.

[8] C.S. Lewis, *The Four Loves*, New York 1960, 92.

[9] Ibid., 93.

[10] Ibid., 93-94.

[11] Ibid., 94.

[12] *Metro* Newspaper, July 3, 2000, 18.

Chapter Four

[1] R. Scruton, 152.

[2] C.S. Lewis, 102.

[3] Ibid., 108.

[4] R. Scruton, 28.

[5] C.S. Lewis, 110.

[6] Ibid., 109-110.

[7] R. Scruton, 153.

[8] Ibid., 131. Italics are mine

[9] Ibid.

[10] Ibid.,136.

[11] Ibid.,144.

[12] Ibid.,138.

[13] Ibid.

[14] Ibid.,139.

[15] J. Bédier, 90.

[16] Ibid.

[17] Ibid.,106.

[18] R.A. Johnson, *We: Understanding the Psychology of Romantic Love*, 102.

[19] R. Scruton, 153.

[20] C.S. Lewis,114.

[21] Ibid.,115.

Chapter Five
[1] S. Freud, "Three Essays on Sexuality", in *On Sexuality*, tr. & ed. J. Strachey & A. Richards, Harmondsworth, 1997, 61.
[2] J. Evola, 12-13.
[3] R. Scruton,140.
[4] Ibid., 145.
[5] A. Carotenuto, 51-52.
[6] A. Giddens, *The Transformation of Intimacy*, Stanford, California 1992, 45.
[7] R. Scruton, 146.
[8] Ibid.,146.
[9] Ibid., 144.
[10] Ibid., 146.
[11] M. Kundera, *Nesnesitelná lehkost byti*, English trans. *The Unbearable Lightness of Being*, tr. M.H. Heim, 20th anniversary edition, New York 1984, II, 15.
[12] Ibid., IV, 15.
[13] Ibid., IV, 16.
[14] Ibid., IV, 17.
[15] A. Carotenuto, 35.
[16] A. Giddens, 45.
[17] A. Carotenuto, 53.
[18] M.S. Peck, *The Road Less Traveled*, 25th Anniversary Edition, 2002, 88.
[19] S. Muto & A. van Kaam, *Commitment*, New York, Mahwah 1989, 74.
[20] F. Imoda, *Lo Sviluppo Umano*, English trans. *Human Development*, tr. E. Dryer, Leuven, Belgium 1998, 133.
[21] A. Carotenuto, 37-38.
[22] Ibid., 39.
[23] Ibid., 38.
[24] Ibid., 80.
[25] Ibid., 82.
[26] Ibid., 84.
[27] A. Giddens, 51.

[28] Ibid., 51.

[29] Ibid.

[30] R. Vannoy, *Sex Without Love: A Philosophical Exploration*, Buffalo, New York 1980, 7-8.

[31] A. Giddens, 59.

[32] Ibid., 60.

[33] S.B. Levine, "Male Heterosexuality", *Review of Psychiatry* 18/5(1999) 34.

[34] A. Giddens, 61.

Chapter Six

[1] A. Carotenuto, 27-28.

[2] Ibid., 27.

[3] Ibid., 28.

[4] Ibid., 52.

[5] L. von Bartalanffy, *General System Theory*, Rev. ed. New York 1969, 71.

[6] See the important book of F. Ferder & J. Heagle.

[7] G. May, *Addiction and Grace*, San Francisco 1988, 1.

[8] A. Carotenuto, 35.

[9] M.S. Peck, 84.

[10] Ibid., 90.

[11] P. Hinnebusch, *Friendship in the Lord*, 60-61.

[12] R. Rolheiser, *Against the Infinite Horizon*, New York 1991, 2001, 51.

[13] Ibid.

[14] M.S. Peck, 89.

[15] S. Muto & A. van Kaam, 75-76.

[16] R. Rolheiser, *The Shattered Lantern*, Rev. ed. New York 2004, 46.

[17] S. Freud, *The Ego and the Id*, The Standard Edition, tr. J. Strachey, New York, London 1960, 47.

[18] Cited by R. Rolheiser, *Against the Infinite Horizon*, 67.

[19] NCCB, *Spiritual Renewal of the American Priesthood*, 2-3.

[20] J. Darlrymple, *Letting God in Love*, Bombay 1993, 8.

[21] C.S. Lewis, 107.

[22] Ibid., 97.

Conclusion

[1] S.E. Stumpf, *Philosophy: History and Problems*, 6th ed., New York, 2003, 62.

[2] R. May, 43-45.

[3] For a detailed understanding of this ideology, see P.C. Vitz, *Psychology as Religion: the Cult of Self-Worship*, 2nd ed. Carlisle, UK 1994.

[4] Thomas Merton has this to say in this regard: "Sanctity is not a matter of being *less* human, but *more* human than other men. This implies a greater capacity for concern, for suffering, for understanding, for sympathy, and also for humor, for joy, for appreciation of the good and beautiful things of life. It follows that a pretended 'way of perfection' that simply destroys or frustrates human values precisely because they are human, and in order to set oneself apart from the rest of men as an object of wonder, is doomed to be nothing but a caricature". See his *Life and Holiness*, New York 1963, 24.

[5] R. Rolheiser, *Against the Infinite Horizon*, 61.

www.ingramcontent.com/pod-product-compliance
Lightning Source LLC
Chambersburg PA
CBHW021341290326
41933CB00037B/331